On Inland Waters

Susan Peterson Gateley

Passages On Inland Waters

Copyright 2004 by Susan Peterson Gateley
All rights reserved. No part of this book may be reproduced in any form or by any means, including electronic without written permission from the publisher.

ISBN: 0-9646149-2-8

Published by Whiskey Hill Press 12025 Delling Rd. Wolcott, NY 14590
susan@silverwaters.com

Acknowledgements

This project would not have been completed without the assistance of others with an interest in maritime heritage, Lake Ontario and other waters. There are many collectors of history who remain anonymous but whose contributions helped preserve these stories. To those known and unknown who have posted to websites, clipped or copied news stories, or who have passed things on, my thanks. Thanks especially to Richard Palmer and Robert Townsend (a special thanks to Robert for republishing Schooner Days columns) to Don Richardson, Lucille Flack, Edgar Denton and others of the Sterling Historical society and the village of Fair Haven who passed on stories, and thanks to Captain Dan for lunch aboard the *Roman*. And special thanks are due to Buster for building the boat basin, *Titania's* happy home these last few seasons.

All photos by Edna Williams are copyrighted and are used by permission and should not be reproduced without written authorization from June MacArthur Spanish Main Dr. #71 Summerland Key FL 33042. The original cover art is copyright 2004 by Irja Cantori.

Passages On Inland Waters is copyrighted 2004 by Susan P. Gateley Contact the publisher for permission to reproduce any portion of this work.

Once again this project like many others, would never have been completed without the tireless technical support team at Cykic Software!

This book is dedicated to my dear shipmate Chris who made it possible.

Table of contents

Introduction   7

Chapter One Jesuit Journeys   9
Chapter Two Marie's Flight   24
Chapter Three The Great Gale of 1880   41
Chapter Four An Erie Canal Passage   51
Chapter Five Lake Ontario Shipping News   66
Chapter Six An Island Passage   78
Chapter Seven Never Say Oops   94
Chapter Eight Old Salts And Bay Sailors   108

Photo Section

Introduction by June MacArthur   120
Photos   124

Additional Readings on Lake Ontario   141
Author Bio   144

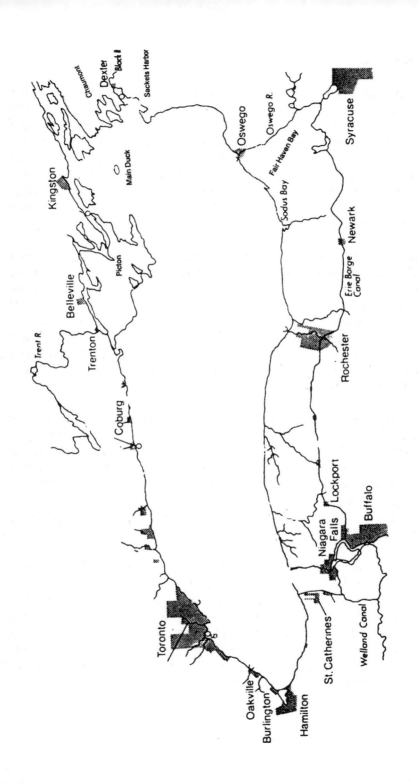

Introduction

Many passages have been written and countless passages made upon Lake Ontario. Some have been undertaken in the hopes of gaining wealth (or at least a paycheck), some for simple curiosity. Some passages have been about military victories, others were quests in search of a short cut to China trade goods. This collection of passages includes cruises made by the author as well as others historic and contemporary. All involved a vessel of some sort, a pleasure boat, freighter, schooner, or bark canoe. Several involved the use of yachts, the type of vessel that today most often plies the lake.

We who sail and who then recall our adventures in word or print follow a literary tradition that undoubtedly predates Odysseus. Passages have been written or told on passages made in probably every sea faring nation's language. Lake Ontario's own literature goes back more than 300 years (with, of course, a far older Native American oral history before that.) Contemporary sailors tell tales of sudden squalls not unlike those of the Jesuit travelers of 1670. And though today's Lake Ontario mariners mostly sail its waters on summer weekends, the elements of wind and water have changed very little from the time of LaSalle.

Yachts and people and the ways in which they interact intrigue me. The relationship between a yacht and those who sail her is complex. A yacht is a place as well as an object. For some, she is a symbol of freedom, adventure, or perhaps of material success and achievement. A yacht is also sort of a state of mind that one enters into when afloat. It is a different place where the scenery changes daily and weather is always of greater interest than what's on TV tonight or the content of the latest batch of e mail.

People interact while on a yacht. Spouses sail or squabble together, friends party or visit or conduct business. Family reunions may involve a yachting excursion. So do some divorces. And people work to achieve a common goal on a yacht, that generally being to get somewhere. Occasionally the yacht's company shares danger together. Life lessons are learned. Sometimes lives are changed forever. When it's over the sailboat's cockpit is often a place of conversation. It's relaxing and pleasant to be afloat and safe in a peaceful anchorage and talk and stories flow then as easily as the water moving past the boat's hull.

I hope those who do sail upon the lake will enjoy reading of other ways and times and of some reasons that have prompted voyages. And I hope that those who have not sailed here themselves will enjoy taking passage on this humble literary bark to voyage with Jesuit and modern day mariner alike.

Note on photo section from June MacArthur

As I've worked with Edna Williams' photos over the years I've come to realize how much she loved the waters around Fair Haven. She photographed every body of water she could get to- the creeks, Fair Haven Bay, Lake Ontario, waterfalls from Watkins Glens to the mighty Niagara. She photographed them in every season, from budding spring, late fall, to ice covered winter. If she had been born in a later time, she probably would have traveled the world taking pictures.

But instead, she quietly took pictures of a small village on the lake. She had one child, a son that she helped raise as an aunt would. She showed us this child and this village as it grew through her box cameras. When the lake and rail shipping industry was bigger than it now is, when planes and the automobile were in their infancy, she made it all look so innocent, so simple, so beautiful. We know it wasn't. But she passed on her love of the water to her son, who passed it on to me. Publishing her pictures is my way of thanking her for everything she did.

Jesuit Journeys

Between 1610 and 1791 the Catholic Church compiled a remarkable series of letters and reports concerning Canada. They are known as *The Relations* and other documents and were written by Jesuit missionaries who were sent over from France to save souls by converting the poor ignorant savages of the New World into enlightened Christians. The effects of contact between the good fathers and the Huron and Iroquois were frequently fairly horrendous for both sides but many passages have been already written on that. Whatever the various outcomes of their work, the missionaries were brave, devoted to their cause and incredibly hardy sometimes working (and writing their dispatches) under extremely harsh conditions.

The Relations were periodic reports sent home to help rally support and financial donations for the church's continued presence in the New World. The missionaries wrote vivid detailed accounts of their travels, the Indians they worked with, and of the land they lived in. Luckily for those of us ignorant folk who speak only our native tongue the *Relations* now translated, are at http://puffin.creighton.edu/jesuit/relations/. In reading them I found these educated dedicated "special forces" soldiers of the church to be likeable men who were deeply dedicated to their cause without being fanatics. Though they often wrote of tragic events, occasional bright moments of friendship and surprising tolerance briefly shine through the shadows of a sad time when two cultures clashed and much blood was shed.

The Jesuit *Relations* contain several accounts of early voyages upon Lake Ontario and adjacent waters. The following is of a voyage upon Lake Ontario in 1656 made by Father Claude Dablon (who has a point just south of Cape Vincent named after him.) Dablon along with Father Chaumonot was on his way to spend a winter with the Iroquois in a village on Onondaga Lake. He sought not only converts to Christianity but also to establish peace between the Onondaga and the decimated Huron allies of the French.

The fathers and their party of Indians and French set out on October 7 to travel up the St. Lawrence. It was hard going paddling, portaging and trekking through the shortening days of fall, and by the 14th their provisions were growing meager so they stopped to hunt. Game was scarce, but they did come upon a "wild cow" (possibly a moose). "That poor animal had drowned, and her flesh smelled very badly; but appetite is an excellent Cook, who, although he flavored this dish with neither salt, pepper, nor cloves, yet made us relish it highly." The very next day their luck turned as they killed eight bears.

They reached Lake Ontario after negotiating the rapids of the St. Lawrence and the Thousand Islands region ."Furious rapids must be passed, which serves as the outlet of the Lake; then one enters a beautiful sheet of Water, sown with various Islands distant hardly a quarter of a league from one another. It is pleasant to see the herds of cows or deer swimming from isle to isle. Our hunters cut them off, on their return to the mainland, and lined the entire shore with them, leading them to death whithersoever they chose."

On October 26 Dablon wrote "We entered the Lake itself proceeding seven or eight leagues. Such a scene of awe inspiring beauty I have never beheld-nothing but islands and huge masses of rock as large as cities all covered with cedars and firs.

"On the 27th, we proceeded 12 good leagues through a multitude of Islands, large and small, after which we saw nothing but water on all sides. In the evening, we met a party of Sonontouaronon (Seneca) hunters, who were eager to see us; and, in order to do so more at their ease, they invited us to a feast of Indian corn and beans, cooked in clear water, without seasoning. This dish has its charms, when flavored with a bit of genuine love."

On the morning of October 29 the travelers reached the mouth of the Salmon River known to Dablon as the Otiatangue, a river that flowed through a region of meadow and marsh and islands just before reaching the lake. "Such is the richness of this stream that it yields at all seasons various kinds of fish. In the spring, as soon as the snows melt, it is full of gold-colored fish; Next come carp, and finally the *achigen*. The latter is a flat fish, half a foot long, and of very fine flavor. Then comes the brill; and, at the end of May, when strawberries are ripe, sturgeon are killed with hatchets. All the rest of the year until winter, the salmon furnishes food to the Village of Onontaé. We made our bed last night on the shore of a Lake where the natives, toward the end of winter, break the ice and catch fish, or, rather, draw them up by the bucketful."

The first run of gold colored fish Dablon describes is probably that of the yellow perch, followed perhaps by the suckers whose mouths resemble those of the carp of Europe that Dablon knew. (Carp had not yet made their way to the New World). The a*chigen* is surely the bullhead, which is a rather compressed "flattened" fish, and brill might be the walleye.

Dablon continues "This was our first lodging in the country of the Onontaeronnons, who received us with profuse demonstrations of friendship. A score of Hurons, who were here fishing, showed their joy at seeing Father Chaumonot, some throwing themselves upon his neck, others inviting him to a feast, and still others sending him presents. " From here the "black gowns" as they were known to the Indians, traveled overland to the village where they spent the winter converting, baptizing, and trying to make a peace treaty between Onondaga and Huron.

The following spring they returned to Montreal to seek more French settlers for Iroquois land. Departing on March 2nd they ended up slogging through knee deep water, wading through a small river, and plowing through slush and mud on a mild spring-like day making about ten miles. The weather then turned sharply colder and they camped for several days. After the weather broke, they continued on, reaching the shore of Lake Ontario March 7. "We hoped to be able to cross the great Lake in canoes; but, though it was not frozen, its entire shore was so encumbered with piles of snow and great blocks of ice, that it was nearly inaccessible. Accordingly, we made two short leagues along the smooth sand; and, after hunting an incredible number of Bustards, which make their winter retreat there in a little swamp, we made ours in the same place for that night." The bustards may have been wild turkeys as the birds were historically present in this area.

For the next several days the party slogged north along the east end of the lake, sometimes encountering half thawed slushy ponds, other times detouring for rivers swollen by spring melt water. "The ninth was a hard day for us. We proceeded over a frozen Pond, but with our feet always in the water, as the rain that had fallen in the morning was not yet frozen. At length, we reached a fine sandy beach on the great Lake, but were stopped by a deep River, the ice on which was too weak to bear us. We sought all kinds of expedients for crossing, but as we found none, my people called a halt to deliberate on our future course. They spent more than three hours trembling with cold…The result was, that we retraced a part of our steps."

One day they crossed a "vast prairie" sloppy with slush and melt water, and waded through three rivers making only a few miles progress. "In weariness God is strong, and in bitterness we find him indeed sweet" wrote the tired Father at the end of the day. Finding the swamps and marshes too difficult to negotiate, the travelers took to the still frozen ice and hiked across its rough surface taking a direct route between points of land that sometimes led them several miles offshore as the ice "occasionally cracked under us".

After about fourteen miles of dangerous ice walking a hard cold March rain drove them ashore to make a miserable camp that soon was washed out by the heavy down pour. "Our little cabin had become, in a short time, a great pond. We rose, and tried to find a dry place... Under such conditions, wrote Dablon, "a night would seem long indeed, did not God illumine the gloom. At any rate, the most patient were the best bedded. Day breaking, we found ourselves all soaked and in disorder, yet were forced still to have patience; for wind, snow, and rain seemed to conspire to detain us in our wretched position." For two more days they waited out the rain before the weather finally improved and they got underway again.

"We passed all the seventeenth with feet in the water, weather rough, and road frightful. At times, we had to climb with feet and hands over mountains of snow; again, to walk over great ice-blocks; and again, to pass over Marshes, plunge into thickets, fell trees for bridging Rivers, cross streams, and avoid precipices; while, at the day's end, we had made barely four short leagues. Finally, to comfort us, we lodged at an inn where there was neither bread nor wine nor bed; but truly God was wholly there". The next day's entry says simply "we proceeded six leagues." Perhaps the good Father was too tired to write more.

On March 19 the rotting ice opened beneath one Indian and he fell through. Dablon also had a close call as the ice gave way under one of his feet but he scrambled to safety. With the ice melting fast the travelers ran for three leagues fearing to stop lest they fall through. They finally made shore where they were forced to "lie down supperless on a bed of pebbles under shelter of an icy north wind." But at least they were alive, and now upon reaching open water were able to take to a canoe that they found cached. Dablon wrote that in a single day traveling with the current aboard their canoe they made forty leagues, a distance that had taken them the preceding three weeks to travel on foot. Just three days later they reached Montreal.

While water travel was far preferable to slogging over land, the untamed St. Lawrence River was a dangerous waterway especially during spring freshets. Father Simon le Moyne writes of a passage on the river made in bark canoes "For, having entered unawares a rapid of considerable extent, we found ourselves in the midst of its billows, which, meeting with many large rocks, raised mountains of water, and hurled us into an abyss at every stroke of our paddles. Our boats, the sides of which were barely half a foot high, soon shipped a great quantity of water; while our men were so thrown into confusion that their cries, mingling with the roar of the torrent, filled us with visions of direful shipwreck. Yet we were forced to go on, the violence of the current bearing us along, in spite of ourselves, through extensive rapids and by ways never navigated before. Our fears redoubled at seeing one of our canoes swallowed up by a breaker which extended across the entire width of the rapids, and which, nevertheless, afforded the only route ... Three Frenchmen were drowned here... Those who were drowned had received communion on that very day, and had piously prepared for death, without knowing that it was so near; but God, who knows his elect, had lovingly made them ready for it"

Though the land was frequently harsh, the Jesuits often praised the Creator's bounty and the beauty of New France. Father Dablon wrote of the Onondaga lands "Our residence is situated between the 42nd and 43rd degrees on the shores of the little Lake Gannentaa, (Onondaga) which would be one of the most commodious and most agreeable dwelling-places in the world, without excepting even the levee of the River Loire, if its Inhabitants were as polished and as tractable. It has advantages that are wanting in the rest of Canada; for, besides grapes, plums, and many other fruits... it has a number of others, which excel ours in beauty, fragrance, and taste. The forests consist almost entirely of chestnut and walnut trees. There are two kinds of nuts; one kind is as sweet and agreeable to the taste as the other is bitter but, with all their bitterness, an excellent oil is extracted from them by passing them through the ashes, through the mill, through fire, and through water, in the same way as the Savages extract oil from sunflowers.

" The most vivid scarlet, the brightest green, the most natural yellow and orange of Europe pale before the various colors that our Savages procure from roots. I say nothing of trees as tall as oaks, whose leaves are as large and as open as those of cabbages; or of many other plants, peculiar to this country, because as yet we are ignorant of their properties."

One of the most detailed and vivid descriptions of pre-colonial Lake Ontario and its surrounding lands comes from the journal of Pierre de Charlevoix, a Jesuit who visited Canada by order of the French government to seek out information on boundaries and routes to the western portion of the continent. Charlevoix followed in the wake of the early missionaries arriving around 1720. He was already familiar with the Quebec area as he had taught at a seminary there in 1705 and he was a scholar and teacher rather than an evangelist, so he had a different perspective on the wilderness than the earlier authors of *The Relations* whose mission was to save souls. Charlevoix also had the option of waiting until May to set forth on his voyage.

Historians tell us Charlevoix was a man of broad background, familiar with cultures and countries far beyond the borders of France and New France. While one historian, Francis Parkman, calls him "unreliable" (Parkman in his writings often seems to have had a bias against Jesuits) Charlevoix was a keen observer and accurate recorder of natural phenomena, and many of his insights and descriptions ring true to this day. Because of his exceptional accuracy and detail his journal has been translated and reprinted and is widely available.

He journeyed up the St. Lawrence, crossed Lake Ontario, coasted along the south shore to Niagara Falls and ultimately continued on down the Mississippi and from there on to the Florida Keys. Like the earlier missionaries, he often wrote of the richness and beauty of the area and its plentiful wildlife. (He did, after all, travel here during the spring). He described the land of the Iroquois by Lake Ontario as "exceedingly delightful" where "The white and red oaks raise their heads as high as the clouds, and there is another tree of a very large kind, the wood of which is hard but brittle and bears a great resemblance to that of the plane-tree; its leaves have five points, are of middle size, of a very beautiful green in the inside, but whitish without. It has got the name of the cotton-tree (possibly the sycamore) because it bears a shell nearly the thickness of an Indian Chestnut-tree, containing a sort of cotton "

Elsewhere he describes another tree that he called "whitewood" (perhaps the basswood tree) that grows to a great thickness and very straight. It is good for planks and boards and the Indians peel the bark to cover their cabins." Another tree he commented on along the shore was the poplar that "grows commonly on the banks of the rivers".

Charlevoix also took interest in the various food plants used by the Indians. He mentions the very common "soleil" (Jeruselum artichoke or sunflower) found in and by their fields and describes another plant also common in the clearings near their villages, one that some folks still find tasty today. "It sprouts like asparagus to the height of about three feet and at the end grow several tufts of flowers. In the morning before the dew has fallen off, they shake the flowers and there falls from it with the humidity a kind of honey which by boiling is reduced to a kind of sugar. The seed is formed in a sort of pod which contains a very fine cotton." This is surely a description of the milkweed, a native plant of sunlit recently disturbed ground. While I've never tried to make a sweetener from milkweed flowers, the edible buds and tiny pods appear on my dinner table each summer as boiled vegetables and presumably the Indians ate milkweed also.

Like most wilderness travelers of the day Charlevoix's party used canoes to get around. The canoe had by then assumed its familiar lines made famous by the fur traders of the 17th and 18th century, a vehicle notes one historian that was to Canada as the covered wagon was to the U.S. The French were never as generally skilled in building the canoe as were the Algonquins, but they quickly caught on to the task of handing these vessels in currents and white water. Eventually the French built canoes up to forty-five feet long. Charlevoix probably traveled in a much smaller model paddled by two or thee men though even in his time canoes capable of carrying 4000 pounds were being built. The use of sails on canoes was apparently then common on the lakes.

Charlevoix wrote that the canoe builders used thick pieces of bark and extremely thin timbers of cedar-wood. "All these timbers from head to stern are kept in form by little cross bars, which form the different seats in the canoe. Two girders of the same materials, to which these bars are fastened or sewed bind the whole fabric. Between the timbers and the bark are inserted small pieces of cedar, still more slender than the timbers and which for all that contribute to strengthen the canoe..." He added that the two extremities of the canoe "are perfectly alike; so that in order to go backward, the canoe-men have only to change offices. He who happens to be behind steers...and the chief employment of he who is forwards, is to take care that the canoe touch nothing that may break it." The canoes under sail could make twenty leagues a day, about 40 to 50 miles, while with "able canoe-men" under paddle they traveled up to twelve leagues a day.

The voyageurs were legendary for their hardiness and strength, one observer writing that they maintained a rate of forty strokes a minute hour after hour. With such energy expenditures of perhaps 5 or 6000 calories a day, it's hardly surprising that that they ate heartily, usually twice a day. As Charlevoix chronicles, they ate everything they could get in their cooking pot including fish, birds of any kind including eagles, bear, porcupines, squirrel and deer along with dried peas corn, and other traveling food.

Charlevoix's party started out in early May from Montreal after the spring freshets had subsided to some degree. Of course, at this time a series of rapids lay west of Montreal and tidal water. The first was "Les Cascades" at the west end of Isle Perrot. Down bound canoes usually ran it noted Charlevoix, but up bound voyagers had to portage. The next barrier was " a fine sheet of water falling from a flat rock of about a foot and a half high." Beyond lay a stretch of white water and minor rapids with "The Cedars" at its head and three leagues from that a fourth rapid. Then came Lake St. Francis, where the party dropped and split one of their canoes while portaging. Though relatively fragile, Charlevoix noted that the birch canoe was readily mended with available roots and gum.

At Lake St. Francis Charlevoix heard the eerie cries of loons for the first time while sleeping ashore. He wrote that "in the night was awakened with piercing cries as of people making lamentations. I was frightened at first, but they soon made me easy, by telling me that it was a kind of cormorants called Huarts from their howling. They also told me these howlings were a sign of wind the next day, and it actually was so." After the lake, the travelers had to negotiate Le Moulinet, a cataract Charlevoix notes that terrified him merely by its sight. The Long Sault a "half a league in length" came next. Some of the lesser white water stretches were dealt with by poling the canoe or by lining it from shore.

On May 8 the travelers experienced a light snow and the temperature was "as in France in January". But the most difficult part of the river was near its end as seven leagues above the Long Sault they reached Le Rapide Plat and beyond that the last white water where a creek called La Galotte entered the St. Lawrence. After that their passage was straight forward with the steady one to two knot current of the big river against them. "We passed through the middle of an archipelago called the thousand islands and I am fully persuaded there are above five hundred of them."

Despite rapids, portages, split canoes and other obstacles Charlevoix's party reached Catarocoui, present day Kingston, after just ten days, traveling on the last day until 3 am in the morning. The party then rested for several days at the fort, before setting out again on May 14 to cross the lake. Six leagues (perhaps 12 to 15 miles) to the west he wrote was the Island of the Roebucks, where a good harbor capable of receiving large barks lay. However, shortly after getting underway from Catarocoui, Charlevoix wrote that "The sun having melted the gum in several places" (on the hauled out canoe) it admitted the water on all sides." The party hastily beached on a convenient shore, perhaps on Amherst island to make repairs and then paddled on. Perhaps a westerly wind slowed them or perhaps Charlevoix underestimated the distance for they never reached the Island of the Roebucks though they continued until "past ten at night".

They camped ashore "at the corner of the forest" and here Charlevoix noted vast numbers of vines in the forest. "I am told this continues all the way to Mexico. These vines are very thick at bottom and bear great plenty of grapes which however, are no larger than pease, but this cannot be otherwise, seeing they are neither pruned nor cultivated. When ripe they afford excellent feeding for the bears who climb to the tops of the highest trees in quest of them."

The party set out early the next day and by 11 am had reached the island "aux Gallots" located, Charlevoix says, three leagues beyond the island of the Roebucks with its good harbor. After a break ashore, they traveled another league and a half to gain the "point of the traverse" (the point of crossing). Charlevoix notes that had he hugged the shore the distance would have been "above forty leagues" adding that this is the route that must be taken whenever the lake was not very calm. "for it be ever so little agitated, the waves are as heavy as those at open sea". From Galloo Island (Isle aux Gallots) Charlevoix wrote "you could see the river of the Chauguen (Oswego River) at a distance of fourteen leagues" across the open lake.

In trying to retrace his route, historians say French leagues could be anything from two to four of our miles. The location of the island of the roebucks "six leagues west of Kingston" eludes me. Because Charlevoix says going straight to it instead of hugging the shore saved him considerable distance one wonders if he set a course for Stony Island or Main Duck and from there traveled to Galloo. Stony Island does have a rift down its middle that could indeed be a harbor where a sizeable "bark" could anchor. Main Duck Island also might have been their destination with its several coves on the north side.

The next morning the Jesuit overrode the concerns of his more experienced guides and opted for a dash across the open lake. A light easterly breeze was blowing off shore, it was clear with the distant blue rise of Tug Hill visible in the distance, and the canoes were evidently rigged for sailing for Charlevoix notes the wind was just sufficient to fill our sails. "The beauty of the country which lay on the left hand did not tempt me, any more than the salmon and great quantities of other excellent fish, which are taken in the six fine rivers, which lie at a distance of two or three leagues from one another. We therefore bore away and till four o'clock had no reason to repent it; but then the wind rose all on a sudden and we should have been very well pleased to have been close in with the land."

After a stiff struggle against the southerly wind and rising waves the travelers made landfall at the Creek of Famine an hour or so before sunset. "It was high time we should arrive" noted the author. Charlevoix and his companions were relieved to be safely ashore even if the Creek of Famine had a bad reputation and feel about it. He wrote that the air seemed "extremely unwholesome". Historians have debated the location of Famine Bay and the associated creeks as being variously on or near the Salmon River or the Black River. It seems likely from the timing of this excursion that this particular Famine Creek was near the south end of Mexico Bay.

Charlevoix describes the land near the lake as being low lying and sandy "for the space of half a league" adding weight to the idea that the landing was closer to the Salmon than the Black River. And the low lying land might have included extensive marshes which even in 1720 were well known to be sources of malaria "mal (bad) air".

The wind continued to blow the next day and on May 16 Charlevoix wrote in his journal with uncharacteristic crankiness, "Here I am detained by a contrary wind...keeping me above a day in one of the worst places in the world." While weathered in and waiting, he hiked along the creek bank and by the lake and in so doing, observed and wrote about a seiche in action. It's one of the first written descriptions of a seiche on Lake Ontario. He described it as "There is a sort of flux and reflux almost instantaneous. The rocks near the banks being covered with water and uncovered again several times in the space of a quarter of an hour." Upon inquiry, Charlevoix learned from his companions that this flux was common and occurred on the other Great Lakes. After reflecting upon it for some time he concluded that a combination of springs at the bottom of the lake and the inflow of rivers "from all sides" somehow produced "those intermitting motions" that he had seen.

Despite the mid May date, Charlevoix also commented on the lack of leaves anywhere upon the shoreline trees. "There is not as yet so much as a single leaf upon the trees though we have sometimes as hot weather as with you in the month of July". Undoubtedly slowed even more at the lake's east end by cool onshore westerlies, spring was slow in coming in 1720. About a week later he wrote of sleeping in the bottom of a canoe and being subject to a "severe frost".

While camped by the hungry river Charlevoix probably watched some of the abundant fish runs passing upstream. Perhaps suckers, bullheads and even sturgeon ascended the clear waters. He also wrote that "there are eagles here of a prodigious size" and that some of the group found a nest and pulled it down "in which there was a cart-load of wood and two eaglets, not as yet feathered". The two eaglets, about the size of small pullets were promptly placed in the cooking pot and served for dinner, though apparently Charlevoix passed on eagle as he wrote "They have eaten them and declare they were very good."

Early accounts of explorers in the area often refer to eating, not surprising I suppose, given the energy expended to paddle 20 to 30 miles a day in a time when travelers had to live off the land. Early travelers, ate swans, "bustards", herons, and all sorts of ducks, "turtles" (turtle doves birds that presumably were later called passenger pigeons), small song birds, and just about anything else that flew that was big enough to shoot or slow enough to club.

After a day the wind dropped and the party got underway happy to leave the shores of Famine Creek. It was a fine day and the lake "was as smooth as glass" as the group shoved off and started west staying a bit offshore. By mid morning the canoes had the Oswego River abeam and a few miles beyond that, Charlevoix recorded that a "small breeze at northeast" arose, and so the party was able to make sail. Running before the light wind, some ten leagues past Oswego they reached the Bay de Goyogouins (Bay of the Cayugas, today Little Sodus Bay). Charlevoix wrote of the shoreline consisting then as now of eroded drumlin bluffs and small embayed swamps and marshes west of Oswego "The whole coast in this tract is diversified with swamps and highlands somewhat sandy, covered with the finest trees especially oaks, which seem as if planted by the hand of men."

Just as the little flotilla brought the Bay of the Cayugas abeam a "strong gale" of wind sprang up from the south so the travelers hastened into protected water. Charlevoix wrote of the bay this writer now calls homeport "This is one of the finest spots I have ever seen". He added that on the left as he entered the bay there lay a cove with a small island which concealed the mouth of a river used, he notes, by the Cayugas to travel from their villages to the lake.(see map). Bear in mind that Sterling Creek, like all the south shore creeks then had a forested watershed and a steadier and more abundant flow than it does now. It was surely more river-like then. Even today, with a bit of portaging around old dams and log jams, a canoe can travel many miles south on Sterling Creek. And the number of Indian artifacts including arrowheads, axes, and net sinkers, found around the bay confirm that the Cayugas did camp on its shores in summer.

After a few hours the wind dropped and the group set out again traveling "three or four leagues" further" before pulling up onto the shore for the night. Presumably they camped a few miles beyond Port Bay. On May 19 they set out before sunrise and traveled another five or six leagues before a brisk northwester moved across the water darkening the lake with ripples and then with waves. Charlevoix's party pulled ashore and camped at a place he calls Riviere des Sables. Possibly this was the site of present day Pultneyville whose creek was well known to fur traders.

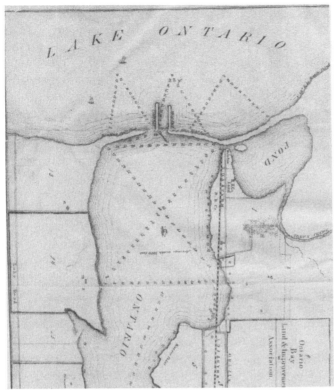

The Bay of the Cayugas, now Little Sodus Bay

Stopped yet again by wind Charlevoix, normally a pretty upbeat chronicler of the beauty and interest of his surroundings, was not a happy camper as he wrote of the hazards of losing ones life by the caprice of the winds and of being stranded by weather on some "barren shore". After three weeks of steady travel through wilderness country since leaving Montreal Charlevoix was growing tired of taking his "lodging under some canoe" and of the perils of seeking shelter ashore in a gale only to risk "being crushed to death by the fall of some tree". He wishes for a proper sailing vessel for travel upon the lakes even as he acknowledges "the trade must be better" before such a thing could happen. It was years before LaSalle's little ships would sail the lake taking workers and hardware to Niagara Falls to build the ill fated *Griffin*.

From the Riviere des Sables the party set out before sunrise the next day and made good time until once again a westerly sprang up in late morning and blew them off the lake. They entered the bay of the Tsonnonthouans, after passing the Genesee River which he noted was narrow and shallow at its entrance and where "two leagues from its mouth two closely spaced waterfalls blocked navigation. Charlevoix wrote that "the bay of the Tsonnonthouans is a delightful place: here is a fine river which meanders between two beautiful meadows skirted with hills, between which you discover valleys which stretch a great way, the whole forming the noblest prospect in the whole world, and is surrounded with a magnificent forest of the tallest and largest timber trees" but the soil seemed to me a little light and sandy." Since he says that the river with the waterfalls was about half way between the Riviere of the Sables and this bay, he was presumably west of Rochester, perhaps around Oak Orchard or Wilson. From this location they traveled a day and a half to reach the Niagara River.

Here Charlevoix and his fellow travelers rested for a day or two before continuing on west on Lake Erie. Here, too, he toured the falls which he noted were not six hundred feet high Father Hennepin and Baron Hontan's descriptions not withstanding. Our analytical Jesuit wrote "My first care after my arrival was to visit the noblest cascade perhaps in the world but I presently found the baron de la Hontan had committed such a mistake with respect to its height and figure as to give grounds to believe he had never seen it...." Nonetheless, Charlevoix found it an impressive cascade that he estimated not less than a hundred and forty or fifty feet a pretty fair guess. A contemporary source gives the Horseshoe Falls height as 161 feet high so Charlevoix's estimate was pretty close.

Even if Niagara wasn't 600 feet high as Father Hennepin le Grand Menteur (liar) had said, the great cataract with its noise "resembling that of thunder at a distance" and its mists that "one would take for smoke" made an abundant impression. From here Charlevoix passes on to the west of our sphere of interest, yet he left behind a portrait of an unbroken nearly unspoiled natural world that today is very difficult to imagine.

Charlevoix, the seasoned international traveler, wrote of that world that when the weather was fair on the lake it was a place of great beauty with water "as clear as that of the purest fountain." During one pause by the sweet water sea he reflected that a life of vagabonding was well suited to make a traveler realize "that we are no more than pilgrims on the earth, and that we have no right to use but as passengers, the good things of this world: That the real wants of man are very few in number, that little is sufficient to purchase contentment, and that we ought to take in good part those evils and crosses which surprise us..." He adds that long voyages are said to be "seldom attended with a large crop of divine grace;" but that in his own experience (at least during good weather) such travel produced an abundance of divine grace.

"Were we always to sail as I then did, with a serene sky in a most charming climate, were we sure of finding everywhere secure and agreeable places to pass the night in, where we might enjoy the pleasure of hunting at a small expense, breath at our ease the purest air, and enjoy the prospect of the finest countries in the universe, we might possibly be tempted to travel to the end of our days."

Marie's Flight

This story is based on an incident that occurred within Lake Ontario's watershed in 1647. Though I've taken some artistic license with the retelling of Marie's passage, I've stuck to the main events as set down by the Jesuits in *The Relations*. Her overland route is not described exactly so it is my imagination that guides her along the lake's eastern shore, though this was a route known to the Indians. Marie was one of several Indian women that successfully fled and found their way back to the Christian settlement that year, but only Marie arrived well fed and in her own canoe. She seems to have been an extremely determined and resourceful young woman who twice escaped from her captors.

Marie's people, the Algonquin, were allies of the Huron and went to war with them against the Iroquois on a number of occasions. The Huron lived north and west of Lake Ontario at the southern edge of the Precambrian shield where a land of infertile unforgiving rock stretches away to the far north. They were skillful farmers and fishermen speaking a language related to that of the Algonquin with whom they shared a common cultural heritage. For a century before Marie's flight, both tribes had been at war with the Iroquois.

Marie lived in a turbulent and tragic time. Her people had been swept by repeated plagues for twenty years and their population devastated. Three years after her journey to freedom, the Huron and Algonquin had been completely scattered by war and disease. Weeds grew in the cornfields that Marie's Huron neighbors had tended in 1647, and the houses of her native village rotted in silence. A proud capable and enterprising people all but vanished, early victims of the clash of European and Native American cultures. A few remnants of Algonquin and Huron, converted to Christianity settled along the St. Lawrence under the protection of the French.

At the time of Marie's capture much of Lake Ontario's watershed seemed little changed by the presence of European traders. But economic forces far from the lake's shores combined to alter the lives of Iroquois and Huron alike. The various Indian tribes of North America had traded among one another before European contact. Virginia clams and tropical conch shells came to upstate NY, copper from Lake Superior came east and the Huron traded with tribes to the north exchanging their corn for skins and dried meat from those whose harsh homeland soils and growing seasons did not support agriculture. But the European lust for beaver quickly changed trade patterns.

The Huron who lived in the strategic middle ground between western tribes and the first French settlements along the St. Lawrence established themselves as middlemen controlling the flow of fur to the French. They eagerly sought iron cooking kettles, steel hatchets, knives, and firearms. These they received along with the Jesuits who journeyed to all reaches of Huronia to spread the good word. The missionaries and couriers de bois also spread viruses and bacteria.

As early as 1611 the Algonquins were struck by an epidemic. More followed. Smallpox, influenza, and childhood diseases like diphtheria, scarlet fever and whooping cough killed over half the Native American population within a few years. In 1634 the first great pandemic of smallpox swept through Huron and Iroquois villages alike. A year later a deadly flue epidemic raged through the St. Lawrence Valley reaching the Hurons by September. In 1639 another smallpox plague struck, and in 1640 *The Relations* state, "Of a thousand persons baptized since the last *Relation,* there are not twenty baptized ones out of danger of death." This was the greatest killer plague yet. In 1645 "maladies succeeded one another" followed by famine. This is hardly surprising, for how could fever weakened farmers and hunters hope to cultivate or harvest their crops and gather and store food for the winter?

The Jesuits were as quick to note the connection between disease and European contact as the Indians were. One priest wrote "since our arrival in these lands, those who had been the nearest to us had happened to be the most ruined by the diseases." The author then writes of Huron retaliation against missionaries for bewitching and cursing them with plagues noting "wherein truly it must be acknowledged that these poor people are in some sense excusable. For it has happened very often…that where we were most welcome, where we baptized most people, there it was in fact where they died the most."

After the Dutch established a trading post at Albany and began bartering for beaver with the tribes of New York and New England, the Mohawks gained control of the fur flow from the west just as the Hurons had done north of the lake. By 1640 the beaver were extinct commercially within Lake Ontario's watershed and the Iroquois had to look further west and north for pelts. But the Huron blocked the fur trade. The two tribes engaged in a series of battles and thanks in part to better access to firearms from their Dutch trading partners, the Iroquois eventually got the upper hand. The Mohawks struck at the French and their Huron allies in a series of raids along the St. Lawrence River. It was during one of those raids that Marie, a recent convert and wife of a Christian Algonquin named Jean Baptist Manitounagouch was taken prisoner and our story begins.

Marie glanced uneasily off to the side of the trail and then looked down at the little girl beside her. Despite the blue sky and the strong light reflecting off the snow on this bright late winter morning, a sense of unease weighed on her. Ahead were the backs of a dozen men, women, and children walking down the hard packed trail. Though a hint of spring was in the air, a series of Iroquois raids along the river in recent weeks had left Marie especially nervous. She had been a prisoner in an Iroquois village as a teenager a few years before. She had then been seized and marched to an Onondaga village only to be freed a year later through the efforts of the Fathers.

Marie heard a slight sound and turned to see the rear guard warrior being seized and stabbed by two Mohawks. A dozen more attackers then materialized out of the shadows of the forest at her shout. Just ahead, her husband's adopted kinsman Bernard Wapmangouch, himself from a Mohawk village, blocked a thrusting lance intended for Jean and then split his assailant's skull with a mighty blow of his war club. But five more warriors closed on him stabbing and slashing as he went down.

She was trying frantically to push her daughter ahead of her toward a dense growth of small hemlocks nearby when she felt an iron grip on one arm followed by a savage wrench that nearly knocked her to the ground. She turned to see a bristling scalp lock and a war painted face contorted by rage, and as the Mohawk yanked her backwards she recognized Bernard's brother. He, too, had once been adopted by her people.

"Pierre!" She gasped. He twisted her arm savagely and snarled "I am Ackameg now. Pierre is no more". Dizzy with pain, Marie turned away from his hatred and saw their party was lost. Every brave including Jean was down. Even as she saw this, a Mohawk was bringing his war club down on her husband's skull. She looked away from blood-splashed snow seeking her child and struggling in Pierre's hard grasp. He shoved her towards a small cluster of women children and a few wounded and disarmed men commanding "Get over there with the others."

With swift efficiency, the raiders then turned to the task of finishing off the severely wounded and killing the children too young to keep up with the forced march to captivity. Marie closed her eyes but heard the shrill scream of her daughter suddenly cut off as the child died under a single smashing blow.

In a blur of shock and horror, she scarcely felt the bite of the leather strip as Pierre bound her wrists tightly behind her. She heard the gasps of victims and yells of conquerors as the Mohawks hacked off fingers to prevent the surviving male prisoners from using a weapon against their captors. The girls, women, and smaller boys were spared this precaution as the war party was in obvious haste, quickly forcing the prisoners into a ragged line and loading them with packs and pouches of plunder.

Pierre came striding back along the line to bind her to another woman. She turned to ask Pierre "Your own brother died by your hand?" "I told you I am Ackameg and my brother was a traitor." After the briefest pause he added. "It is better that he died quickly." Marie, realizing the truth of that, asked "Are you taking us to your village?" Pierre grunted assent. "Is Father Jogue still there?" Pierre's face darkened. "The French witch was killed. He cursed our village and our corn became infested with worms. He brought death to our children with his holy water poison. " Marie's heart sank as the forked limb was lashed to her neck. What hope had any of them now if these devils would kill even the blessed Father who had come in peace and without weapons to their village.

They marched at a forced pace throughout the bright cold day and at dusk joined forces with the camp of another war party and more captives. The bruised and battered prisoners were shoved together, and Marie saw many of her neighbors. What would be their fate? She had escaped the eaters of flesh once, would she be so lucky a second time? Among the prisoners was Tawichkron baptized Jean, once a leader among his home village before converting to follow the word of the missionaries. Tawichkron had been badly beaten. Huge bruises and oozing cuts and wounds covered his arms and legs, and the Mohawks had stripped him of his outer clothing. But seeing Marie, he met her gaze straight on and gave her a brief nod. Then Tawichkron got to his feet and turned and said in a calm strong voice to the huddled prisoners. "Courage. Be strong my brothers and sisters. Let us not forsake our Faith or prayer. Our enemies will soon pass away and our torments will be brief before Heaven becomes our eternal dwelling. God has not abandoned us."

Marie felt a sudden lift of spirit. Here was Tawichkron with his mutilated hands and battered body standing as straight and proud as a tall pine among them. Was it not so that her innocent child must now dwell loved in Paradise? She joined the other prisoners as Tawichkron led them in prayer. Tears flooded Marie's eyes as the familiar words were murmured around her. The Iroquois hearing their voices and seeing them bowed in prayer started in amazement, and then a young brave near Marie laughed derisively. Marie finishing the prayer straightened and looked squarely at Pierre now Ackameg and said loudly. "Tell your people you must not mock a thing so holy. It is our custom to pray to God and he will punish those who despise him"

The youth guffawed and leaped forward pulling his knife and raising it above her face. "Let your God stop me from drinking your blood !" But Marie stared him down, raising her hand to make the sign of the cross before her slowly and deliberately. The silent prisoners behind her imitated her. Pierre, suddenly shamed stepped forward and knocked the knife aside. "Leave them. They are sheep and their prayers are harmless. We are not afraid of them and shall let them pray as they wish for now."

Ten days later the footsore weary prisoners reached the Mohawk village. All knew their time of greatest trial now lay ahead. Marie had seen it before, the burning, beating, and slow torture of men and boys hacked to pieces bit by bit. And this time was no different. Your 21st century author will spare you the details of the slow death of Jean Tawichkron, and other details of the torture of the male prisoners. It's in volume 30 of *The Relations* and it took Tawichkron twenty hours to finally make it to the Paradise he believed awaited him. Torture and human cruelty haven't changed a lot in 300 years, and Marie had every reason to believe that she would not be spared from being a "plaything in the flames" as so many of her companions were that winter night in 1647 in central New York.

Shortly after that dreadful night, two visiting Onondaga recognized Marie, once a slave in their own village. They took her aside at dusk and said that she should return to service for she was their rightful slave. To

Marie it was as if God had truly touched her life. Slavery was preferable to burning, and she agreed to go with the two men the next morning. They set out then along the Indian trail that follows approximately the track of Route 5 and 20 today. After several days travel, they came to the land of the Oneida and spent the night in their village. Here, the Onondagas told Marie to wait outside the palisade for them. They feared losing their just acquired slave to the Oneidas. They left her with scanty clothing and a handful of provisions in a pouch to the frosty night telling her "we'll be back for you in the morning."

It was cold that early March night with a brittle wind whimpering among the bare branches that clacked and clattered overhead. Marie clad in just a light cape over her short tunic was restless, hungry, and cold. Defying her captors' instructions she crept cautiously forward toward the cleared area near the palisaded village and then stopped to listen to a conversation between two teenaged Oneidas walking the trail towards the village gate.

She strained to understand their dialect, somewhat like that of the Onondaga she had been enslaved with. She heard one youth laugh, caught something about a feast, about food, and then heard her own name. Had the Oneida's learned of the Onondaga's captive? She leaned forward and held her breath straining to concentrate on the accented words and heard "the slave". Then "which part of the body do you like best?" "The feet roasted under the ashes-they're very good."

Panic knotted Marie's stomach. They were going to eat her. She would be hacked to pieces, thrown into the fire, cooked, and devoured. She crept carefully away from the clearing, and then bolted for her hiding place and meager cache of food. Something had gone wrong. The Onondagas were going to give her to the eaters of flesh. She had escaped them once before, and they would never allow her to live for a second chance to humiliate them. She must escape, now. She must go as fast and as far as she could starting this moment.

After the first surge of panic, Marie forced herself to calm down. She walked quietly back to where the pouch of food awaited, took it up and began striding down the trail to the east, retracing her steps. They would not expect her to walk toward the land of the Mohawk's on the hard packed trail where they could never pick out her tracks. But she must travel fast through the night to get as close to the village she had left two days before as possible. Then she would seek a hiding place near it and lay up.

Though the small skin she wore over her shoulders and her short dress were thin, she did not feel the cold as she jogged along the level trail. And with the warmth of her flight, she felt the faintest stirring of hope also rising. If she could avoid the Iroquois until they gave up searching for her and then slip away to work north, she might be able to return to the settlement along the great river. Already she was thinking ahead determined to escape again, this time on her own with no help from anyone.

Marie trotted steadily though after several hours her leg muscles ached and cramped and she felt as if she had a large stone tied to each leg. The wind dropped after midnight, and the clouds moved away so the waning moon lit her path with a pale silvery light on the snow. The temperature dropped with the wind and when Marie stopped to scoop up a bit of snow for her parched throat, her breath formed a luminous cloud before her. She stood then, her pulse sounding in her ears as she tried to listen for any sign of pursuit. Nothing stirred in the forest. She heard only the rasp of her breath and a distant owl hooting- the owl, attendant to the dead. She shivered and wondered if Jean was in Heaven with their daughter this night. Almost too faint to hear the keening howl of a far away wolf reached her. Jean's totem had been the wolf. Was he calling her to join him? Her sodden feet were beginning to ache, so she started down the trail again. If she could reach the Onondaga village before daylight and find a secure refuge and lay up, they might not find her. Who would think to search for her so close to the camp of her enemies?

As the first light of dawn began to pale the sky and wash out the stars in the east, Marie slowed to a cautious walk. Ahead of her lay the open fields around the Mohawk village, luminous with snow and early morning light. A few dried corn stalks stood dark against the snow. She turned back into the forest seeking a refuge to spend the day among the dense cedar and spruce thicket she had noticed perhaps a quarter mile back. She descended into the low lying area, still iced over and then used a bough to brush out her trail as she worked slowly into the thicket. Dawn found her curled tightly in a meager bed of spruce and cedar boughs, surrounded by the thick growth of evergreens. Despite her wet feet and the cold she fell asleep quickly, exhausted by the all night marathon run.

Marie awoke in late afternoon ravenously hungry sore stiff and cold. No one was around so she felt safe in moving about as long as she stayed inside the cedar grove. She opened the pouch and took stock- a handful of parched corn and a half a handful of pemmican. She took the pemmican and chewed it slowly watching the light fade and wondering how long she could bear to linger so close to the village. As she gazed across the field, a few large flakes began to fall from the low overcast, lazy and slow on the still March air. By nightfall it was snowing hard and she felt quite safe to venture out into the field to glean, knowing any signs she left would be covered by morning.

Hours of scratching and digging among the ice and crusted snow unearthed only a hand full of partial cobs from the frozen field and Marie retreated to her spruce bough bed cold and discouraged to spend a second night. This time sleep came far harder, and she kept shivering herself awake.

In the morning Marie was awakened by the sound of village women talking a few yards away. She wished she had hidden further from the field as she could clearly see the women moving past the screen of foliage. Then she saw a tall man carrying a hatchet walking purposely across the field. He seemed to be heading right for her. She kept as still as rabbit, trying to disappear into the tangle of branches around her but she was sure he saw her. Every nerve end tingled as the urge to bolt nearly overwhelmed her. Less than twenty feet from her hiding place the man turned aside and continued on his way. But Marie knew she could not stay near the village any longer. She must move on, away from the scanty supply of corn and into the forest.

As the sun climbed, its strong spring light began to soften the snow and the crust underneath the latest six-inch fall no longer supported her weight. Marie broke through repeatedly and with only the protection of her short skirt and moccasins, her leggings having been taken, her legs were soon reddened with cold and slashed by the icy crust. With each step she sank deep into the softening slush. It seared her bare skin and soaked her feet but after the first mile or so, her legs and feet grew numb even as she left traces of red on the snow. After an hour of struggle she saw a grove of young pines nearby and floundered over to twist off a few branches. From these she fashioned a pair of crude snowshoes, though with no knife to cut a strips for lashing, they were poorly made and soon fell apart.

Fear of pursuit drove her deep into the forest, and she now worked north through the dense growth. Her route took her over a series of ridges and low lying areas and often the valley areas were a tangle of dense cedar and spruce thickets agonizingly slow to work through. Sometimes she encountered windfalls to climb over and through and to detour around and some of the low areas were filled with shallow freezing slushy water. By afternoon of this overcast day she was lost, uncertain even of the direction she now traveled in.

Staggering with fatigue as she lurched through the heavy soft snow, she stumbled and fell occasionally. Her feet were long since numb making it even harder to keep her balance. Now as the gray day began to darken into twilight she was shivering in her soaked clothing. As daylight faded and the trees blended into a wall of darkness around her, Marie staggered into the cover of a grove of young hemlocks. She found a large rotted log with a hollow some dried leaves from last fall had collected. She crawled in and waited for morning.

This night was the worst yet. Sleep was slow in coming as Marie shivered and ached. Finally she passed into restless sleep filled with despair and nightmarish dreams. Again she saw flames and heard the yelps and shrill exultant cries of the Iroquois. Again she saw the cutting and slicing off of flesh from living captives and smelled the burned flesh. Orange flames flickered around her and someone near by was sobbing and screaming. She tried to run through the curtain of fire around her. A slender youth stood before her, he held up his arms in prayer with only charred blackened stumps where his hands had been, his burned bones showing clearly. Then she fled.

She raced over a hard crusted field of snow leaping over bodies lying like logs underfoot. She saw her brother and both her sisters among them. Their faces were unmarked by the plagues that had killed them. The sky in the distance was lit with flame and she stopped and stood on a wide flat expanse of ice. Alone. Then she saw Jean and her daughter on the other side of a dark fast running river. They were both shouting and beckoning her to come. She started to wade in but the current was far too strong and she floated swiftly away as they grew smaller and more distant.

She awoke aching and stiff. Grief for her loved ones stabbed like a knife in her heart. She began to weep, quietly at first, then in loud wails and sobs of misery that shook her whole body. Finally spent, she quieted, and dreading more dreams of fire and blood she sat up against the log and half dozed the rest of the night with her knees drawn up tight to her chin. As she huddled in the night the owl called again and another answered. Back and forth they called. "I am dead. It is over with my life" thought Marie. She could not bear to sleep and dream again, and the thought of another day of battling through tangled logs, slush, ice, and deep snow was all but unbearable. Why? With no one she loved left alive. Why go on? I might meet up with another Iroquois. They'll torture me as an example to the other slaves. It is better to die now quietly and quickly. She thought again of Tawichkron leading the prisoners in prayer so long ago now that seemed. She murmured the prayer, then stood up and looked around in the pale light of dawn.

A tall strong tree stood nearby with some lower branches within reach. She climbed up about twenty feet, worked out on a limb and while clinging to the next one above with one hand took the belt of her dress off and fastened the end around the branch above and made a noose with a slip knot. This she placed around her neck. She closed her eyes and whispered "Jean I am coming" and leaned forward from the branch, lost her balance and fell.

The impact of her drop knocked the breath from her lungs, and she lay gasping in the snow realizing the thong had snapped. She felt the noose biting into her neck and looked up towards the branches and dim gray sky overhead. She felt the snow under her and her sore bruised neck and ribs, and thought "It is not God's will that I die." She stood, reached up and slowly worked the thong loose from her neck, still thinking. "If God wishes me to live there must be a reason. And if he can save my life, perhaps he can help me to find my way home. "

Thinking of the village along the river, her home, and the little chapel there where the women had sung on Sunday mornings she thought also of Chaouerindamaguetch as she called her French teacher and mentor. A luminous patch of snow on a dark log nearby in the growing light of dawn seemed to Marie to take on the look of the Sister's white face. As she gazed at it she felt the nun's love surrounding her like a thick fur robe, warming and strengthening. "She is calling to me to help me find the way" and suddenly she was grateful for her life. "God is good. I must live. The sisters want me to return to the village. There I can still do God's work". In the strengthening dawn light the face faded and became a bit of snow again. But peace settled over Marie as she walked away from the tree that she had chosen to be her executioner.

Dawn whitened the sky in the east and the mush and slush of yesterday was now crusted over and grown hard again, so Marie made good time on this day. When the sun got high enough to soften the snow, she rested and ate the last of the corn that she had gleaned. Already she could feel the change in her body as her flesh began to consume itself. Famine was no stranger to Marie. It had visited her village when she was a child. She knew she must conserve her strength even as she moved onward.

Later in the afternoon she came to an area where the snow was thinner and there were some bare patches of ground. She picked up a stick and tried digging along a small stream bank where the ground wasn't frozen in search of roots. She followed the still frozen stream for a mile or so to a place where it widened out into a pond and here, where a bit of water showed between ice and shore she found in the mud, several clumps of starchy tubers. They were barely edible uncooked, but she chewed on them as she continued walking west and north.

For two more over-cast days with no sun or stars for Marie to take a bearing from, she wandered through dense spruce thickets and the slush and snow of wet and swampy forests in what *The Relations* called a horrible solitude. Although she no longer wanted to die, she was several times near despair when she crossed her own trail after hours of struggling through the forest. On the third day she tried skinning some bark off a pine sapling to chew its stringy fiber. She felt noticeably more tired. She must have food. For over a week she had lived on a hand full of corn and pemmican and a few roots while walking through the day.

Then, after four days of wandering, the sun shone again, and she was able to head north. It was now early April and the strengthening sun melted the snow quickly. As the snow thinned it grew easier to trudge through. The sun also helped her spirits, despite her growing weakness. She felt more determined to go on. And for the first time there was a softness in the afternoon wind that brushed her face with a promise of spring even as her legs became rubbery and weak. It was growing dark when she heard the two crows. They were calling urgently back and forth and she decided, lost as she was, to seek them out. Crow had been her grandmother's spirit bird, and she felt that these birds were calling to her.

She approached the clearing they were calling from and saw one bird swoop down to the ground by a little bush, look in her direction and call loudly over and over. "He wants me to approach" she thought. The bird stood its ground, large and bold and then flew up suddenly to a nearby tree. The she saw it beside the log the crow had been perched on, a rusted bit of metal. She bent down, and to her astonishment picked up a steel hatchet. As she stood up, the crow flapped into the air, called once more and was joined by its mate.

"Thank you" she whispered weakly. But the crows weren't finished. Both birds circled overhead cawing even more loudly and urgently, then both dropped to the ground a few yards away. Marie slowly followed them again. One bird hopped and flapped into the air, repeatedly calling. There, still half covered by snow and frozen, lay the slender legs and grayish body of a winter killed deer. Marie dropped beside it, still clutching the hatchet filled with wonder at her luck. The crow said something loudly overhead and she looked up, then took the hatchet and quickly chopped off two chunks from the frozen haunch and tossed them toward the birds. They flew down and seized the pieces and flapped away.

She wasted no time in making a fire stick, shavings and then a fire. That night she ate meat. After her first substantial meal in nearly two weeks, Marie drew close to the small campfire and placed a few more sticks on it. As she watched the flames she made plans. She would stay here for a couple of days to smoke some of the meat before moving on. Though this little cleared area was obviously a summer camp of the Iroquois, they would not be anywhere in the area for at least another moon yet. She would rest and grow stronger. The flickering fire was such a comfort. Already the memories of her flight and confused wandering were jumbled and fragmentary. The fire made her think of being back in her village as a child, watching Grandmother boil fish in the iron kettle while Mangouch, her favorite dog, lay nearby alert for a handout.

Memories like the shifting flames came and went, her cousins, dead of the coughing disease, her father, and two older brothers, slain by Iroquois, her Grandfather, carried away by the spotted sickness. "Why do I still live when all the others have died or are slaves? I am no more worthy". She longed to see and hear other friendly humans. Then, with a chill, she recalled one of the villagers, Bernard Wapmangouch, confessing his sins just before they had set out on that last fatal journey. He had told the priest "I am called onto the woods to die there. Pray for me, for I shall come back no more." And Jean Tawichkron who had stood up to the Iroquois, he had given a bundle of prime beaver pelts away just before they left. "Are these not thine?" asked the priest. "They are so no longer, for I account myself already dead" he had replied.

And now he was, along with every other man and boy that had walked with her that day. The fire was dying like her nation itself. Marie bowed her head, closed her eyes and prayed for the souls of the dead.

*   *   *

Marie spent the next day finding wood, tending the fire and drying and smoking strips of deer she worried away from the frozen carcass. It was cold and overcast, but there was a hint of change in the air, and in the afternoon the raw east wind gave way to a softer milder south wind. Marie rested another night and day preparing for her trek north and heard the geese for the first time. Their flocks flew by the thousands, like arrows overhead before the south wind. She heard their excited calls and looking aloft said I will follow you to the big river and my people, those that are left. Her spirits soared with their urgent clamor in the sky.

She set out the next day with a warming sun making good time through the thinning snow. Near the end of this day she came to the banks of a fast flowing river. Melting runoff had filled it to the top of its banks, and it hurried past her a hundred feet wide, turbid, and powerful. She turned and worked up stream climbing over and through occasional tangles of brush and windfall, making slow progress before nightfall. She took shelter tired but no longer hungry as she chewed some of her meat. That night she did not dream.

In the morning she decided to seek a crossing point. "Then I'll follow the river downstream to the great lake. It will lead me north if I follow its shore. There'll be no more blind twisting and turning through out the forest then". After about an hour of working along the river she came to a logjam where a huge willow had toppled into the river. She crossed and went down the river. Late in the day she heard a distant sullen roar, the voice of the great lake.

The river now passed into a widening valley. It's current slowed and its banks were fringed with a wide tawny golden marsh. Looking upon the brown stalks of cattails, Marie thought about possible food there. The marsh would be more favorable for foraging than the winter forest had been. She continued along the shore and near dusk reached a low hill that overlooked the river's mouth and the wide gray waters of the lake. The waves were rolling in driven ashore by a strong west wind blowing off the cold water. It cut through her meager clothing like a knife. Row after row of white cresting breakers threw themselves ashore, and to Marie's ears attuned to days of solitary forest living their roar was deafening. As she gazed upon the river's end, she wished for a net. By now fish might be running up the river, and if she only had some sort of net she might be able to catch some. But how to make a net with no material at hand? And she had neither time nor energy to single handedly create a weir of brush and sticks.

She noticed the gulls gathered at the river's mouth flying back and forth shrieking and occasionally diving down to the water. She went down to the beach where she could see they were catching small fish. She decided to fashion a spear. After several hours of standing on the bank as still as a heron and making a number of strikes that missed, she succeeded in spearing two sizeable fish. That night she felt she had enjoyed one of the finest meals she had ever had. For several days Marie followed the great lake's coast north. She also caught more fish with her make shift spear. Finally she realized she must leave the water that had been her friend giving her food and direction and strike towards the big river.

After a few days travel inland, it turned cold. That afternoon a thin veil of ashy cloud blurred the sky and a large rainbow halo shimmered around the sun. "He is in his house. It will rain soon" thought Marie. By afternoon a raw northeast wind moaned through bare tree limbs and the penetrating cold sliced the half naked woman's flesh like a knife. She sought shelter as an icy drizzle began in an outcrop of rock that formed a shallow cave. She huddled listening to the wind that spoke with a hollow sorrowful voice among the trees. It was too windy for a fire, so she dozed and half dreamed of happier times in her village.

But warm weather followed the rain, and the forest was transformed almost over night. Under the April sun creeks and rivers ran bank full. Marie's pace slowed as she foraged for food finding turtles and frogs in the streams and marshes and digging along the banks for roots and tubers.

The first woodland flowers began to appear, bright green pungent leeks, dainty star like spring beauty, and yellow trout lily. Marie cooked only after dark, trying to build fires screened by logs or dense growth of evergreens. She feared the smoke might give her away by day. She wasn't always able to travel in the direction she wished, but though she had seen no sign of pursuit, she felt she must stay off the trails and well worn paths that foraging Mohawk might use. She had little idea of her location, but when the sun shone, she always walked north.

For nearly two weeks Marie traveled an irregular halting path northward. Though nights were still frosty and cold, she now had her fire and the days grew steadily warmer. She fashioned snares, caught a rabbit and continued to find food along the water. Her clothing was tattered and her moccasins were wearing out. She tried cutting some of her cape up and wrapping her feet with it but soon gave it up and resigned herself to going barefoot. At least now she walked in cold mud rather than in ice and snow.

The forest was no longer silent. Grouse drummed and turkeys yelped and called. At night she often slept with the sounds of calling frogs nearby, and she felt less lonely than during the cold still nights of March. Then one afternoon as she walked along she heard men's voices raised in an argument. She froze, looked around quickly for cover, then crept ahead quietly now on alert. Her fears were confirmed. Two Mohawks stood on the bank of a large stream bickering over something. She thought with her imperfect grasp of the language, that perhaps they were debating pursuit of a bear they had seen though she wasn't sure. Of greater interest to her, however, was their canoe.

It wasn't a crude elm bark canoe that the Iroquois normally fashioned. This was a true Huron made birch canoe, large enough and strong enough to carry two or three men and light enough for one to carry. It lay pulled up on the shore, and Marie could hardly believe her good fortune as the two hunters, still arguing, headed off into the forest. She waited a few more minutes listening, then hurried to the boat to see that the paddles were stowed. They were, along with a kettle, blankets, and a knife." Quickly before they return" she thought and with that pushed off into the stream, picked up a blade and began paddling strongly. No more bruised aching feet now. Ahead lay the clear channel and she was certain, beyond that a few days travel was the big river. All she had to do was head down stream for home, taking care to avoid enemy travelers.

Marie put as much distance astern the first day as possible going farther in an afternoon than she had walked in three days. She drew the canoe well up into the fringe of growth by the stream and concealed it further with some branches the first night. She was tired and her arms and shoulders and back ached from the unaccustomed task of paddling. But she was well pleased, for now there would be no more wandering among the dark thickets and giant trees and tangled windfalls of the forest. No more stubbed toes and bruised heels and cut feet either. If she could avoid discovery, all would be well.

Luck was with Marie for the three days it took to reach the big river. But here she watched its strong fast current and occasional large chunks of ice sailing past realizing she would have to wait before continuing on down river and trying her luck with the rapids. A large number of rocky islands and outcrops of granite marked this stretch of the river and Marie decided to stay on one of the islands. She selected a large densely wooded hideaway and settled in. Her new home was about two hundred yards long with much of its shoreline marked by bold outcrops and steep drop offs of rock. One end was low lying and she found a bit of a beach to pull the canoe up on. While she was pulling the canoe out, she was startled by the sudden snort of a deer followed by the crash of its flight into the thicket in the middle of the island. That gave Marie an idea.

She tracked the deer, a yearling, and flushed it and then drove it ahead of her. The deer fled to the island's north end where it was stopped by the steep drop off. It doubled back and as Marie had hoped, ran down to the low end and plunged into the river. Marie ran after it, pushed the canoe off and pursued the deer. At first the animal swam strongly for the nearby shore, but Marie managed to turn it back into the river. Using her tomahawk she struck at the deer's head nearly capsizing. She switched to the spear, using it as a club and trying to force the animal under water. After several tries, she was able to approach the tired animal closely enough to strike it a heavy blow with the hatchet. Then she used the blade to quickly cut its throat. Using what was left of her cape, she lashed her kill to the canoe's end and carefully began to paddle back to the island.

When the struggle was over, she sat for a moment in the canoe shaking with relief. How easily the deer could have capsized her. She looked at it, as it lay still and limp, and felt a sharp pang of regret. "May you find your way safely to the spirit grounds and live there with others of your kind in peace" she thought. She also said a brief prayer of Thanksgiving for having the strength to make the kill and for having the hatchet and the canoe that had made it possible.

As the spring went on the river waters dropped and Marie felt safe in continuing. As she paddled along she passed islands thick with birds and stopped to gather eggs. She passed by a smaller river where she saw the great sturgeon gathering to spawn. Remembering her previous fishing, she fashioned another spear burning the end to make it hard and took several sturgeon and smoked the meat to add to her traveling food. By late May the flow over the dangerous rapids above Montreal had diminished enough to make the last run home.

And so it was around the eighth day of June, a canoe appeared above the habitation of Montreal, in which was seen only one person. Marie arrived at the village of Christians to be greeted with joy and love by French, Algonquin, and Huron alike. "At last, here I am among my kindred." said Marie as she embraced the nuns and the fellow tribes people who welcomed her home.

A Perfect Lake Ontario Storm

On Lake Ontario fall brings strong winds. A few days before this was written a storm in October 2003 generated fifteen foot waves and winds in excess of 80 miles an hour, and over the years such fall gales have claimed many lives- The *George B. Sloan* was smashed on a pier on October 30 1885 drowning one of the crew while attempting to enter the wave swept Oswego channel. The schooner *St. Peter* went down just east of Pultneyville on October 27, 1898 taking all but one with her, and a Halloween blow swept young Moses Dulmage away in his yawl boat from an anchored schooner into the night. But throughout Lake Ontario history November has been the most deadly month.

A dozen or more November storms have made it into the history books. The several gales of November 1880 are among the best documented as they featured several particularly poignant wrecks witnessed by many bystanders. One of these was the schooner *Belle Sheridan* who "In the year of eighteen-eighty on a drear November day with coal bound for Toronto left old Charlotte Bay" as immortalized in a ballad by Mike Ryan.

That year, the month began stormy. On the first, rain and hail swept across the water sinking the schooner *Odd Fellow* with her cargo of shingles off Charlotte and driving the schooner *Tranchemontague* ashore in Oswego. Another schooner the *Marysburg* with barley aboard hit bottom while in tow in the heavy seas over the harbor bar of Oswego taking on water wetting 1700 bushels of grain, while the ship *Bermuda* also while entering Oswego took a sea aboard that threw the icebox through the wall of the cabin and then filled the captain's quarters with water. Late that month another gale claimed the *Wave Crest*, driving her ashore near Frenchman's Bay after her anchor chain parted, and it swept a man off the deck of another schooner. But the worst storm came on November 6 and 7 when five schooners and the steamer *Zealand* went to the bottom.

November has been a lethal month on all the lakes- the Great Lakes gale of 1913, subject of several books, sank over a dozen ships with a loss of at least 250 lives. In November 1966 the freighter *Daniel J. Morrel* sank on Lake Huron, while on November 10 1975 the *Edmund Fitzgerald* went down on Lake Superior with her whole crew. While exactly what happened to that ore carrier may never be known, according to the Coast

Guard's analysis it's suspected that she went down very quickly, perhaps in less than a minute as there were no distress calls or indications of lifeboat launching. It is known that she had sustained damage to at least one hatch cover before her last cruise. Perhaps she struck a shoal earlier and damaged her hull or perhaps leaks through the hatch from the heavy seas continually washing over her deck allowed many tons of water to mix with her cargo adding weight and making the pelletized ore more prone to shift and slosh around in her holds. Then there came one last wave, the one she couldn't lift to. The condition of the wreck as it lies on the bottom suggests that she made a sudden final plunge, perhaps speeded by a massive abrupt movement of the water saturated cargo as it sloshed forward to help drive her under.

Both economics and meteorology contributed to making November a particularly lethal month for mariners on Lake Ontario. The shipping season traditionally ended on the lakes by December because of ice and lack of insurance coverage, so the urge to squeeze one or two last trips in to try to push the bottom line over a little further into the black before the long winter lay up was in constant conflict with good sense and bad weather. And in November weather patterns shift to send more gales our way. In late fall two storm tracks begin to converge over the western Great Lakes. One brings disturbances from the Canadian interior, the other directs lows that form over the mid western plains northward. At the same time the polar jet stream with wind speeds of up to 290 mph often parks over the Great Lakes region.

Any time sharply contrasting air masses come together in close association with the jet stream and with each other the potential for violence exists as pressure differences try to rapidly even out. When the gales of November came to Lake Ontario in 1880 the scenario might have been somewhat as follows; Perhaps around November 5 a low pressure system made up of warm air saturated with moisture from the Gulf of Mexico moved north. As it neared the lakes the low deepened with its swirl of circulation tightening even as another storm from the north dropped down over Lake Superior. As that low moved over the unfrozen water it picked up a significant energy boost from the vast reservoir of summer heat still stored in Superior's depths. It could well be that in 1880 these storms merged (as we know happened in the great gale of 1913) and then combined their forces. The strengthening gale then drew even more energy from the polar jet as it was shoved rapidly along and continued to feed on heat released from the lakes below it. By the time the storm hit Erie and Ontario on the night of November 6 it was screaming. At least a half dozen ships died on Lake Ontario alone that night.

The southerly winds began light that morning and the air had an oppressive almost muggy feel. At least two schooner men elected to stay in port that day C.H.J. Snider tells us in his "Schooner Days" column that ran serially in Toronto's *Evening Telegram*. The captains of the little *Maple Leaf* with a load of barley in Black Creek and the *Sea Bird*, anchored nearby behind Waupoose Island both looked at the low hanging gray clouds and listened to their intuition and the hollow moan of the wind in the bare trees on shore that morning. Then they and their crews lashed down loose gear and secured for bad weather. But elsewhere the *Baltic*, The *Belle Sheridan*, the *Wood Duck* and a dozen other schooners, some making their last trip of the season did decide to get underway. For several ships and their crews, it was their last trip ever.

Schooner Entering Harbor, Fair Haven, N.Y.

Lake Erie just to our west got the storm a few hours sooner. There the wind came on heavy from the southwest and then from the west on Saturday afternoon, and by dusk the temperature was dropping fast as the cold front arrived. A news account of the death of the schooner *Falmouth* near Buffalo quotes her mate S.D. Becker as saying of that night "It was blowing a strong gale...and it was intensely cold, every drop of water that touched the rigging or spars freezing almost instantly." That night heavy snow squalls swept both Erie and Ontario and visibility in blowing spray and squalls was nil. Out on the lake amidst waves that roared and snarled past their ships like small hills in the darkness schooner crews struggled on icy decks in the bitter wind to reduce sail and steer down the lake running for cover. The blast from the southwest pushed the waters of Lake Erie before it in a storm surge that raised the water level gauge at Buffalo ten feet or more, while ships settled into the mud in Toledo harbor near the lake's west end.

Aboard the big carrier *Baltic* on this day loaded with lumber, as on other Lake Ontario ships, the crew, noting the falling barometer was busy shortening sail at dusk. But the storm waited until the wee hours of the night to unleash its full fury on the lake. At midnight the already strong wind began howling with hurricane force with speeds over sixty knots tearing off large limbs and uprooting trees on the high bank under which the *Maple Leaf* was huddled. That same wind went roaring and screaming through the rigging of her sisters on the open lake. Steep breaking twenty-foot waves rolled down the lake, occasional "freak" waves loomed ten feet above these. The *Baltic* was now frequently spearing deep into the seas with her jib boom, a part of the ship normally angled twenty feet above the water when she was on an even keel.

C.H.J. Snider wrote that the boarding seas washed her deck load of lumber over, the heavy planks flung off only to thump along the ship's sides as she ran them over. It took the mate and three men two hours to lash down the flying jib out on the end of that wave washed jib boom. "The maddened sail would blow out and in the thick blackness of the early morning you would see the sparks fly from the chain pennants of the thrashing job-sheets."

The waves that pounded the *Baltic* were vicious close spaced killers, characteristic of the relatively shallow waters of the Great Lakes. Such waves with only a seven or eight second period wave length give loaded ships little time to lift, clear their decks and recover before they are boarded by the next sea. About a century after the gale of 1880 yacht racer Ted Turner, veteran of some of the roughest ocean yacht races around, competed in a Chicago to Mackinac race on Lake Michigan and saw waves that he said were some of the worst he'd ever experienced.

The Baltic ran nearly the whole length of Lake Ontario that night to make for Kingston. The next morning with most of her canvas in tatters and much of her rig tangled and fouled, she staggered to safety. Snider wrote that her crew spent a week refitting their ship. Other schooners came into port similarly battered and glazed with four to six inches of ice. And still others were less lucky that wind swept night and never made it to any port. One of these was the ill fated *Belle Sheridan* whose demise was vividly told by Snider in his "Schooner Days" as well as in contemporary news accounts.

Some of the ships that have been lost on Lake Ontario went down on dark waters with no survivors, no witnesses and no one to tell the tale of their passing. But others like the *Belle Sheridan* were driven ashore only to be smashed to pieces a few hundred feet away from horrified bystanders who were helpless to render aid. Dozens of schooners were lost on Lake Ontario in the nineteenth century in this fashion. Sometimes they went down only a few yards from the safety of a harbor or breakwater. All too often crew members drowned, died of exposure, or were simply battered to death on the very doorway of a harbor or safe refuge.

One of these, the schooner *Garibaldi* was swept ashore on the southwest shore of Prince Edward County just a few days after the *Belle Sheridan's* loss. Like the *Sheridan*, she tried to anchor, but her cable broke and she too drove into the surf. Two of the crew stayed aboard overnight and says a contemporary news account "the next day "They had to be chopped loose from the ice." One man was dead, frozen solid standing up the other, her captain, lost both feet from frostbite and exposure. When the *Belle Sheridan* went ashore near Bald Head, town of Consecon, the surf was so violent that that the lake literally tore the bodies of the victims apart. An old news account says "portions of viscera" were found along the beach the next morning. Among the body bits, wrote Snider was a human heart. Wreckage was spread from Wellers Bay to aptly named Wicked Point within a day or two.

The *Belle Sheridan's* death in the gale of November 6-7 1880 is one of Lake Ontario's better documented tragedies, partly because it was well witnessed. Snider devoted at least two columns to the disaster and when he was publishing Schooner Days in the 1930s and 40s old timers along the Prince Edward County's southwestern shore still recalled the wreck. The *Sheridan's* violent end is also remembered because she was a family affair, commanded by James McSherry and crewed by his sons Johnny, James Jr., Tommy and Eddie, just 13 years old but already working on the family ship. One other sailor, Sam Boyd, manned the schooner, and her mate was from Toronto. The *Belle Sheridan* was an Oswego built two master, 123 feet long on this day she sailed with three hundred tons of coal from Charlotte bound for Toronto on a glum Saturday morning with the same fluky southerly that made the *Maple Leaf's* young skipper uneasy enough to stay in port. Teen aged crew notwithstanding, there was ample experience aboard the *Sheridan,* as Captain McSherry had commanded schooners for a number of years in the stone, cordwood, and coal trade. Although far from new, the *Belle Sheridan* launched in 1852 had been rebuilt and was classed by the underwriters as B-1, sound enough Snider, notes, to carry perishable grain cargoes.

The Belle Sheridan sailed along the south shore making her westing toward Toronto with the offshore wind throughout Saturday. But at about 11 o'clock that night, her captain, watching the fast falling barometer, ordered his sons to shorten sail, and at midnight near Thirty Mile Point the first blast of the storm front hit, strong and vicious from the southwest. Though the ship could then have possibly sailed on a close reach for her destination, the wind was so powerful McSherry decided to scud before it under short sail. The schooner steered east by north angling across the lake, and an hour later as she ran in fast building seas, the mainsail tore to shreds. The flogging tatters caused the thrashing spars to break. Seas were now boarding and sweeping the decks of the deep laden coal carrier as she rolled almost under bare poles. At 3 am the violent motion snapped one of the topmasts off, and the crew cut away the dragging spar and its rigging. Now the captain hoped to make Presquile harbor at dawn. But without a mainsail, his ship was barely maneuverable and when her crew tried to steer into the shelter of the bay behind Presquile Point, she simply went sideways driven down on to the waiting lee shore.

McSherry let go both anchors and with the worst of the seas broken by the point to their west, there was hope that she would hold. For a few hours she did, but then one anchor chain, perhaps chafed by the violent motion, snapped. With the full strain now on a single anchor it began to drag slowly and inexorably across the mud and rock ledge bottom. Two hours later the ship struck. The crew crowded up onto the highest portion of the grounded vessel, swept by the bitter cold wind that had now swung into the north and savagely pounded by the surf and spray. They were perhaps 500 feet from land and safety. Four Prince Edward County locals attempted to launch a boat and reach the wreck, while other farmers and fishermen stood by on shore hoping and praying for rescue. The heavy breakers capsized the would-be rescuers, but after they washed ashore, they righted their boat bailed it out and tried again.

Repeated rescue efforts were in vain. All but one of the *Sheridan's* crew were lost. A news account says that first the father Captain McSherry died. Later Edward cried out several times that he could stand it no longer and died in his brother's arms. Perhaps figuring he had no other choice, the sole survivor, James Jr., took up a plank from the deck and seeing the rescue boat get clear of the surf on yet another rescue attempt he jumped into the icy water. The strong along shore current swept him east parallel to shore, but the rescue boat crew rowed after him. More than a mile to leeward the crew finally reached him and hauled him to safety. He was the only man saved despite valiant efforts to reach the schooner to bring off the rest of her crew. As the Oswego paper reported "shortly after James reached the shore, the mainmast gave way and fell directly across where the remainder of the crew were holding. After this event, the survivor knows little beyond the fact that they perished, one after another."

In the same gale that destroyed the *Belle Sheridan* another schooner also went ashore near by. This was the two-master *Albatross,* who blew ashore with a load of shingles and lumber and an estimated 150 tons of ice on her topsides. Her crew was rescued, but the ship soon broke up. And sometime during the night the wooden steamer *Zealand* went down off Prince Edward County near Nicholson Island. She took 14 people with her and the loss was not discovered until November 9th when the schooner *May Taylor* came upon a mass of floating wreckage and a smashed stove in lifeboat.

At Oswego the gale also took its toll. Here not one but two schooners went ashore during the gale. In both cases the crews got off with no loss of life. The little *Wood Duck* carrying 4700 bushels of barley for the malt houses of Oswego, made it through the night, but the heavy seas and current from the river along with the wind made entering Oswego harbor without a tug impossible. The tug tried to get to her in time and managed to heave a light line aboard, but in the rough seas the crews were unable to secure the heavy hawser in time to tow her in. So she swept past the piers and went ashore within fifty feet of high water. *Wood Duck* drove so far onto the beach that her crew climbed out onto the jib boom and then dropped off onto the land according to one account.

The Oswego Palladium wrote of the "gallant effort" by the tug *F.D. Wheeler*, under command of C. W. Ferris, to reach her in time but alas, swept by heavy seas and constantly awash, the *Wood Duck* had lost her primary towline out on the open lake. As her captain recalled in the news article after the first miss, "we began drifting down the lake sideways but the tug to our surprise came for us again and this time got our line." But the jury rigged tow line was too short and said the captain "there was a kink in it" and the line before it could be secured "ran off the timber head". The tug had nearly beached herself on the second attempt to reach the fast drifting schooner and there was no room for a third attempt. The *Wood Duck*'s Captain told the newspaper reporter "I think the tug did nobly, coming almost too far for her own safety; Twice she filled with water and we could not see her."

Another Canadian schooner, the *Snowbird* loaded with lumber, went ashore a few yards away a couple hours later. Her crew was rescued by the life saving service and she was sold for salvage. Surprisingly, she was later hauled off the beach and the tough old ship lived to sail many more years and eventually fell apart in a backwater of Toronto Harbor. But the *Wood Duck* was a total loss.

Oswego harbor at the time of the November 1880 gales

Nineteenth century Oswego was a particularly dangerous harbor for unpowered sailing vessels to enter during heavy weather. Back then the break waters didn't extend out as far into the lake, so the current from the river was felt far more than it would be today. Sometimes in the fall after heavy rains the current ran six or eight knots or more. And in a westerly gale waves had the whole length of the lake to build up in before they hit shore here. The action of the river current and the refraction and reflection of the breaking seas in the shallows as they bounced off the jetties made for a confused steep chaotic sea much like a tide rip that all too often flung the schooners violently off course and sometimes smashed them into one of the jetties. Or some ships struck the river bar in the troughs of the waves and ripped their bottoms out. Leo Finn's book *Old Shipping Days* lists dozens of schooners lost at Oswego. Some missed the entrance and went ashore on the rock ledges just east of it under Fort Ontario.

A third gale hit Lake Ontario two weeks later creating more havoc for the lake's already battered and hard pressed schooner fleet. Almost immediately after the blow, an intense cold snap froze harbors and canals. By the 24th the Welland canal had six inches ice on it, and many ships were caught where they lay and had to winter in far from homeport. It was in this storm that the *Garibaldi*, a 200 ton two master built seventeen years before and loaded with coal before went ashore not far from where the Sheridan had been pounded to pieces. The Oswego Palladium reported that this parting shot from November's wind gods tore away canvas, put ships ashore, and dismasted schooners on both lakes Erie and Ontario. One vessel, the schooner *Mystic Star* was so iced up that though within twenty miles of the Welland Canal, she could no longer beat up wind and had to run the whole length of the lake with bare poles. Another schooner lost her yawl boat as it was "smashed into pieces" and ships were iced up as high as the cross-trees of their masts. "The fleet arrived yesterday afternoon and appeared like so many icebergs." reported the Oswego newspaper. It had been a rough year.

But other years were unkind too in the fall. Among ships lost at Oswego in about a ten year period around the time of the 1880 gale, *Old Shipping Days* lists *Kate Kelly*, ashore under Fort Ontario in 1876, The *Gannett* and *Prince Edward*, lost in 1874, the schooners *Ontanagan* and *Coquette* lost near the end of the east pier, the *Baltic* and *Austrua*, sunk just inside the harbor. Just the year before the November 1880 gale the *Hattie Howard*, loaded with lumber from Port Hope tried to make the harbor of Oswego. On November 19 she hit the west pier and "went to pieces. In October 1881 another schooner hit the east pier during the night and was wrecked. Her captain thought he was steering for the end of the pier and its light when in fact heavy waves had extinguished the harbor beacon. The luckless schooner was instead steering for a streetlight when she hit.

And so the long sad roll call of schooners and steamers smashed, sunk, stranded, or simply swallowed up by the lake during the stormy month of November goes. A partial list of victims from the November 6-7 gale of 1880 as culled from David Swayze's database of approximately 5000 Great lakes wrecks, includes the 92 foot two master *Albatross,* the *Belle Sheridan*, the three masted *Norway* (capsized then righted minus her rig, deck load of lumber, and her entire crew) and the *Bermuda,* another grain carrier bound for Oswego but run ashore and lost in Canada. Her crew got off. The aforementioned *Zealand* and *Wood Duck* also were lost. Snider mentions another, the *Thomas Street* also pounded to pieces on Prince Edward County's limestone shore. That November at least ten ships sank or went ashore, eight of them in a single storm.

In 1933 an October gale swept over the gray waters of Lake Ontario, rattling windows inland, buffeting shoreline cottages, and blowing spindrift and spray off the waves. In the morning a beachcomber on the windswept shore of Prince Edward County saw a mass of blackened wood moving inshore through the surf. It was all that remained of the *Belle Sheridan*, given up from its lake grave by the gale. The sole survivor of the wreck, James McSherry, had died a few months before.

"With no response to the friendly hail
Of kindred craft in the busy bay
I shall slip my moorings and sail away-"

A Passage on Narrow Waters

The New York State canal system is unique. Once dozens of canals stitched thousands of miles across the eastern half of the nation. Ohio, Illinois, Massachusetts, Maryland, Pennsylvania - all had man made water highways that carried millions of tons of freight and hundreds of thousands of passengers. Of that 19th century inland network, only one canal still survives in a fully navigable state. The others are mostly mere depressions in a forest or are now filled in with trash or turned into roadbeds. But New York's 534 miles of waterway still connect Buffalo directly with Albany and via the Hudson connect Lake Ontario to New York City and the world beyond. Or you can go north through Lake Champlain to the St. Lawrence and Canada or south into the Finger Lakes' wine country and to Ithaca, the intellectual capital of upstate.

While traveling on it with a boat you feel a strong sense of separation from the daily routine of the "real world" a few yards away. The canal exists in a parallel universe paced with a slower clock than that of normal reality and paved roads. It is a place of tranquility rich in beauty where quiet waters reflect the images of wooded and flower spangled banks. This former highway for commerce is now almost exclusively the path of pleasure craft. Only this small portion of society still knows and uses this road. At the start of the 21st century it's an all but forgotten byway.

Most of us who sail, dream each fall of making at least one long leisurely passage to some distant tropical harbor far from the December winds that sweep Lake Ontario. I'm no exception, having nourished fantasies of heading south to Florida with my yacht for at least three decades, my dreams fueled by Joe Richard's book *Princess,* Sloan Wilson's *Away From It All* and the improbable *Enchanted Voyage* of Hector Pecket in Robert Nathan's novel. But to date the best I've managed in the way of lengthy southern cruises was a journey with my husband aboard our sloop *Titania* in the fall of 2000 to the distant southern city of Baltimore, just over the Mason Dixon line.

This was a five-week trip of about a thousand miles. We went south in the fall, left *Titania* in the care of Fair View Marina for the winter, then brought her back the following spring. And even though tens of thousands of boats like our own have made similar passages and hundreds do it every fall, it was our first time. As the cliché says, it's not the destination but the journey. Along the way there were a few surprises. One of those was how interesting ditch crawling turned out to be.

Upon *Titania's* return during June's long days of lush new growth, the canal seemed almost a dream path. We wandered down a woodsy lane without seeing another traveler for hours at a stretch. Sometimes trees leaned far out into the sunlit space over the brown surface of the canal reaching for the light. You had the feeling that without human intervention the forest would soon swallow the narrow channel up filling it with tangled limbs and branches.

Our pace was slow enough as we moved across the state at 40 to 50 miles a day along with other canal wayfarers for us all to become a loose community of sorts. Soon we were exchanging tips on Laundromat locations and good restaurants and by day three or four you wondered where *Antigone* the home built German steel ketch or *Attitude,* the little trawler from Lake Michigan was now. Lock tenders shared this quiet world with us along with a few state workboats and dredges and their crews and the Canadian "snowbirds". Bass fishermen, party barges and runabouts made up much of the local traffic. Occasionally an out of place tuna tower equipped cruiser or mega yacht swept past, travelers from a different reality than ours. Slow quiet boats made up most of the long distance traffic.

Except maybe for your first lock, the canal is not about adrenalin or high adventure. It's strictly linear travel at a leisurely pace. I could tolerate its linearity and enjoyed its tranquility for a week anyway. Chris thought it was a little boring, but, we agreed, a little boredom in life is not a bad thing. Luckily *Titania's* elderly engine also tolerated it as long as it got a quart of oil each morning. It felt good at the end of the trip to slip out again onto the wide spaces of our home waters and turn back into a sailboat though. Lake Ontario and the St. Lawrence with its path to salt water offer many possibilities for adventure. The canal's offerings are fewer. It helped build Chicago and Manhattan, but today it's a smooth blue byway and backwater.

Our passage began in early September with a short run under power, our mast lashed on deck. With a brisk southwest breeze on a cool morning, the lake was nearly flat though an easy swell running in from the west rolled us along. Two days of southerly winds had blown the summer's warmth offshore so we sailed on icy clear green water with the rocky bottom 30 feet beneath us clearly visible. That cold water helped bring schools of fall run king salmon inshore to the Oswego River where a dozen or so anglers were trolling for them aboard a clustered fleet of small outboard boats at the harbor mouth. The stocked fish, which grow to 40 pounds or more, attract droves of sportsmen from New Jersey, Pennsylvania and New England to Oswego and the lake's east end each fall. By lunchtime we were ready to ascend the Oswego River.

This section of the canal took us from approximately 245 feet above sea level up to 363 feet. This differential today powers several hydro dams producing up to 10000 kilowatts of power along the river, and it also helped turn the wheels of 19th industry at Oswego. At its peak the little Lake Ontario port rivaled Buffalo and surpassed Rochester as a trade and industrial center. Vast amounts of lumber and grain passed through here bound as we were, ultimately for New York City. Thousands of workers labored in the Kingsford Starch, Vulcan Iron Works, or the Oswego Shade Cloth factories along the river. Oswego also played a key role in the French and Indian War and had things gone a bit differently there then, I might now be writing this in French.

For many years Oswego was the only British outpost on all the Great Lakes. Trade in furs flowed east from the upper lakes through Oswego, then down the Mohawk to the Hudson and New York City. Because it was the sole British connection to the western frontier, it was highly strategic and critical to England's tenuous hold to North America's western lands. So it was bitterly contested in the war with France and several major battles were fought here. One of the bloodiest took place in August 1756 when the French moved against Oswego with a force of about 3000 regulars, militia, and Huron and Algonkin Indians, many of them with no love lost for the English. The French working under cover of darkness brought 22 canon up to begin battering the several small riverside forts. After several days, Fort Pepperill's commanding officer was killed by a cannonball, leaving behind a frightened demoralized force of defenders and 140 women and children. Fearing for the safety of the noncombatants, the junior officers decided to surrender, hoping the French would protect them from the Indian allies.

Alas, they didn't, and the Indians followed their usual battlefield practice of torture and revenge, hacking, chopping, and cutting up any one they could get their hands on. At least a hundred prisoners were either killed or scalped including all the wounded and sick in the garrison hospital.

Oswego lay in ruins, deserted by the British for two years. Oddly, the French also failed to occupy it, and the abandoned but still strategically placed post was later used by General Bradstreet to launch a successful thrust against the French. He took Kingston and cleared the way for a push down the St. Lawrence to Montreal and the final French defeat.

The waterway we entered at lock 8 was born of bloodshed, international trading rivalries and fierce political battles. A major motive for digging the first ditch was to create a safer alternative route to Lake Ontario for trade. In 1820 the lake was still a military frontier with a potentially hostile force on the other side. After its completion five years later the canal was truly a nation shaper. By the 1840s over 7000 dollars of tolls a week were being collected on the Erie feeder canal at Oswego alone, and Clinton's Ditch assured that New York City would dominate the fierce rivalry between Boston, New York, and Montreal as chief 19th century east coast port. The canal also funneled immigrants west and north to the then sparsely settled and still disputed prairie boundary with Canada to secure its present location. The first version of the Erie, just forty feet wide and four feet deep, was so successful it was soon enlarged. The current longest duration version was finished around 1917.

The first canal was a conduit for commerce and social change. On it there passed people with fresh ideas and crazy schemes that still influence today's society. Historians say it's no coincidence that the canal corridor was a hot bed of abolitionist activity, religious fervor and that the women's rights movement and one of today's great and still fast growing churches, the Latter Day Saints, germinated in canal towns. Lesser known movements for spiritual and social change like the Fox Sisters with their séances, the Oneida Community with its unconventional ideas of marriage and connubial bliss, and the Fowler brothers' popularization of phrenology also took root or grew and flourished near the canal. Though it isn't the countryside of France, a cruise along the route of the old Erie is in some ways more interesting, for here you travel in the wake of hucksters, idealists, utopians, entrepreneurs, and prophets unique to America.

The canal also nourished a corridor of industrial development and innovation that made this truly the Empire State, for a time the most populous and powerful in the nation, and the only state ever to undertake and maintain a public works waterway of such magnitude. The list of inventions and leading technology developed by a single canal side company alone, the Remington Rand Corporation based in Ilion, is staggering. The first production run of velocipedes (bicycle forerunners), broom and match making machinery, bank vaults, office furniture and office machines to house them, sewing machines, and of course, typewriters all came forth from its factories. Founded in 1816 by a blacksmith-farmer, the company remains in business today making firearms. As Richard Garrity points out in his book *Canal Boatman*, the firearms business out lived both the earlier canals. Somebody somewhere is always needing a good gun. The company may well outlive this canal too.

By its large scale movement of people and goods, the first little water filled ditch helped facilitate a creative outpouring of commerce and capitalism the results of which continue to reverberate around the world to this day even as the canal and upstate countryside around it settle into a contemporary economic backwater. It took 20 years of intense and sometimes bitter political wrangling and the largest state bond act New York had ever then passed to create the present day version of the canal system.

It very nearly didn't happen at all, as by the turn of the century the canal's commercial future was already dimming thanks to competition from the railroads. But then as now some groups feared excessive concentrated corporate power and the canal, seen as competition to keep rail shipping rates in check, was ultimately funded and rebuilt by the state.

Unlike earlier line cut versions, the current canal was created by an intricate process of controlling the water levels of various rivers across the state. This was a major engineering undertaking involving hundreds of culverts, dams, tantor gates, locks, guard gates and other water control structures. A lock tender told me that his lock machinery is a scaled down version of the Panama Canal's and that some of the electrical relays were actually leftovers from the contractor's Panama job. (The Panama locks were constructed a few years before the Erie's last enlargement and it opened in 1914)

Nearly a century later, despite its complexity and the restless shifting forces of nature it must deal with, the waterway continues to work for the most part pretty smoothly. When you enter your first lock and hear the groan of the doors closing behind you and look at the white jets of water spurting along the sill as tons of river press against the steel looming over head ready to burst in and drown you in an instant, your regard for the work of those now forgotten artisans and early 20th century engineers rises with the water beneath your keel.

Locking through was generally pretty painless, though the first time was interesting. We approached slowly waiting for the traffic light by the lock gates to turn green. We then glided into the chamber's dank depths. A certain sense of fatalism was in order as the massive steel gates closed astern with a low thud that echoed off the surrounding slime covered cement walls. Our lives were now at the mercy of 95 year old machinery designed by long dead civil engineers. Then a sudden boil 20 feet across erupted behind the boat and, the water began to rise lifting *Titania* and her crew with surprising nearly silent speed into the sunlight. It was good to see the geraniums in the lock side flowerbeds and feel the sun's warmth as the water leveled out and grew still again and the gates swung open to release us.

After passing through the Oswego River locks, we spent a quiet drizzly night at the "International Port" of Phoenix's newly refurbished little canal side town park. Directly across the street was a handy Red & White with two cruising staples ice and beer. From here we passed through the Three Rivers section, a pretty stretch of wandering channel that goes by upscale waterfront homes, modest cottages, and many miles of wooded banks with occasional islands and weedy backwaters populated with herons and egrets. The next town, Brewerton today is a busy little recreational canal port, home to several full service marinas able to haul out large yachts. Sometimes long distance cruisers and retirees will leave their trawlers stored here for the winter and go off home to their Florida or California homes for a break ashore.

We entered the wider waters of Oneida Lake by late afternoon and on this warm September day the lake was mirror calm, reflecting cumulous clouds to our north in its polished surface. It was also under going a spectacular blue green algae bloom. The water looked like a solid green painted surface beside us as we plowed through it, even our bow wave and the wakes of passing power boats were dyed green by the unfathomable numbers of tiny single celled plants.

Shallow thirty mile long Oneida Lake has a reputation among canal travelers with low powered sailboats for kicking up a disagreeable steep chop in a moment's notice. But that same shallow water also makes Oneida Lake a great fish producer. Until its commercial fishery was closed down, over 300 tons of perch and sucker were taken from the lake each year and fish pirates set illegal nets for decades after netting was banned in favor of sport fishing. One local history recorded that as late as the 1950s "fish pirates" were still netting on Oneida Lake and that at least one Brewerton church mortgage was paid off by fish pirate contributions.

The lake also once hosted a tremendous eel fishery. The place name Caughdenoy, just west of Brewerton was said to mean "where the eel is lying down" in the language of the Oneidas. These oily fleshed fish were well suited to preservation by smoking in pre refrigeration days and were a vital winter food to Indian and early settlers alike. In 1653 a Jesuit missionary wrote "the eel constitutes a manna exceeding all belief" and noted that thousands could be speared in a night. Eels were speared with long spears tipped with tines of ash or tamarack root. The eel would coil around the tines of the fork and after retrieval the fishermen would step on it to pull it off the spear. As late as 1928 a hundred tons a year were taken from Oneida Lake tributaries but canal construction blocked the runs to salt water and the last eels were fished out in the late 1930's. Of that great multitude, none now remains.

On the calm hazy September day of our first voyage upon Oneida Lake I had ample time to look around at the scenery. I noted near the channel several small low lying rocky islands some with strips of plastic tape shimmering in the sun rigged from stakes, presumably to discourage the fish eating cormorants so despised by anglers from nesting here. One was identified on the chart as Wantry. According to one account, canal surveyors changed its original name of One Tree in 1913 so as not to confuse canal navigators since by then the one tree was gone. Admittedly, even allowing for disappearing trees, canal navigation might not be considered a highly rigorous art by an old seadog, but Oneida Lake with its 8 to 10 mile wide expanses seemed downright oceanic after a day or two of ditch crawling where the shore is never more than a few boat lengths away. We paid close attention to the closely spaced markers as we chugged along for the lake has several rocky shoals near the channel.

We spent the night in the little resort area of Sylvan Beach. After dinner attracted by the rattle of the roller coaster cars, we wandered over to the little amusement park for an ice cream. I've never seen an emptier park than this one was on a mild early fall Friday night. People were all at home playing computer games I guess.

I enjoyed the vintage carousel with its colorful wooden horses, rabbits, rooster, zebra and antelope. Brightly lit and playing a merry tune it twirled in the night, with nary a rider aboard. We watched the Ferris wheel go around a few times, ate our ice cream and went back to the boat. Clearly Sylvan Beach's golden age was firmly in the past. Back when the owner of the Vaseline Company built a big hotel here in 1899 the annual hop growers' picnic drew 20,000 people who came by excursion train. Even after the age of the auto, people still came to Russell's Hotel and Danceland to dance with Ellington, the Doresy's and Glenn Miller. I wondered as we went back to *Titania*, how much longer Sylvan Beach would hang on before it perhaps shared the fate of another waterfront amusement park I knew of in the region- torn down for condos and waterfront mini mansions.

The next day *Titania* in her houseboat mode, hummed along past Rome and Utica and on into the Mohawk Valley making six knots. About ten thousand years ago the last glaciers receded from New York, and prehistoric Lake Iroquois formed roughly where Ontario is now. For a time while the St. Lawrence outlet remained blocked with ice, all the waters of this inland sea flowed eastward through the Mohawk Valley. At Little Falls, an old canal town jammed into narrow gap between two highland areas, a huge waterfall larger than Niagara once carved a passage from a fault line in the raised area.

This was one of the few breaches on the entire eastern coast of the Appalachian and Adirondack Mountains that made westward travel and commerce so difficult in colonial days. Because of that barrier, the English clung to coastal settlements for a hundred years while the French, using the Great Lakes, penetrated deep into the heart of the continent. And because of the Hudson and Mohawk River highway, the Dutch established Albany as a fur trading post six years before Plymouth Rock's settlement. To this day the Mohawk Valley remains a major transportation corridor. For several hours we traveled a few yards away from a busy railroad line and from the New York State Thruway. As we steamed along over serene brown waters thousands of cars and hundreds of semi's roared past. Sometimes a trucker, perhaps a bit envious of our leisure, tooted at us and one train engineer gave us a wave as he went by.

In 1873 the author of a Harpers magazine article on the canal compared it to the then rapidly expanding railroad system stating that each boat carried on average more than most railroad trains. "Yet it has well been said that while the plodding canal-boat attracts no attention, the railroad train creates a sensation in every village through which it passes. Standing in the roadway or sweet meadowland, attention never rests upon the boat that is gliding through the narrow inland waterway..." It still feels that way most of the time. The boat usually slips past canal side towns, cow pastures, and back yards with little fuss or notice.

We stopped that night in Little Falls and tied up in the early dusk of September, glad to silence the engine after a long day during which we covered less distance than an hour's journey by auto on the Thruway. Little Falls is a place of trains coming and going. Their racket and whistles echoed off the hillsides that draw in close here while the quiet murmur of the rain swollen river falling over the dam just downstream and the steady chant of late summer insects told of the season moving on.

Little Falls is an old mill town that boasts fewer residents now than 50 years ago, but it is working hard to reinvent itself as a port of call for tourists. We enjoyed our stay at the one time state department of transportation canal terminal transformed into an attractive waterfront park offering free 30 amp power, showers, and restrooms. A 15 minute walk across the bridge over the river gorge was downtown and its super market, restaurants and handy Laundromat. We spent a rainy day here, Chris working aboard while I explored.

Little Fall's history goes back to the early 1700's when a small settlement grew up at the portage around the falls. Later, hydropower ran dozens of mills and factories, and the city prospered. Today a stroll along some of the streets on the north side heights over the river takes you past the impressive brick and stone houses of the factory owners that still look proudly down on the rest of town. The lower lying south side of the valley was where the factory workers lived in rows of modest wood frame residences huddled in the shadow under a nearly vertical 600 foot high wall of dark gray rock.

Little Falls was Asteroga (rocky waters) to the Mohawks who came to its whitewater cataracts to fish the vast runs of Atlantic salmon ascending from saltwater. Later the Palatines followed the water up into the valley and settled at the falls by the 1720s. Like Oswego, this was to be a hotly contested and blood drenched battleground during the French-English war with frequent raids by the French and their Algonquin allies to burn and kill. But the fertile soil of the river valley encouraged rapid rebuilding, and Mohawk Valley wheat and corn were critical in sustaining American armies during the Revolution. Some of the earliest locks in the country were built here in 1796 to get around the falls.

Waterpower, the canal, and agriculture fueled the little settlement's rapid growth. By Civil War days foundries, knitting mills (that turned out thousands of Union Army uniforms) starch factories, and planing and saw mills stood along the river. This was also an early base for the Remington Rand Company, makers of typewriters, punch card adding machines and filing equipment in the early 1900's. (The Remington Arms continues making guns to this day just down the canal a few miles). In the 1920s and 30's Remington Rand went head to head with another upstart punched card tabulating machine maker, IBM of nearby Endicott and lost. No one today remembers the "ENIAC's" of the Mohawk Valley. And a 1964 high tech breakthrough by Mohawk Data Services of using magnetic tape instead of paper punch cards to store information never caught on. Instead of turning the Mohawk Valley into Silicon Valley, Mohawk Data quietly slipped away into oblivion in 1990 as someone else successfully marketed magnetic storage and the local economy drifted into the 21st century with housing prices at about a tenth of the going southern California rate.

The city's historical museum occupies a onetime bank with its massive limestone walls now protecting early bicycles old photos Herkimer diamonds and other artifacts. The vault remains firmly grounded on solid bedrock so nobody can blast in easily. One display detailed the Little Falls Cheese Market. During the economic surge of Civil War brokers from many states and cities came here to deal in cheese. Herkimer County exported over ten million pounds of cheese a year and 600,000 pounds changed hands in a day on this Wall Street of cheddar. At first the traders gathered to make deals on a street in an informal outdoor market near the present day historical society. Later this was the largest cheese market in the nation, with much of the product going to New York and other east coast cities. Little Falls supported a large cheese making infrastructure making wooden boxes, hardware associated with handling cheese, rennet, and "dandelion" cheese coloring pigment.

The whole enterprise dried up, if you'll excuse the pun, when large scale fluid milk transport via the railroad became feasible. Before that time milk was essentially a "waste" product, for farmers sold only cream. Cheese was a way of preserving and transporting a product that would otherwise have been unmarketable.

However, the rugged rocky Adirondack foothills just north of Little Falls still lend themselves to dairy farming, and the underlying limestone and dolomite that sweeten soil and encourage the growth of good pasture forage for cows also gave Little Falls another claim to fame, that of the Herkimer diamond. You don't wander around town for very long before encountering at least one example, and the museum had several collections assembled years ago by local gem hunters. Hundreds of sparkling clear sixteen facet naturally formed "diamonds" that look like cut gems glittered and sparkled in the lovingly arranged displays. To this day diamond "mines" cater to tourists who cheerfully pay good money to break rocks for a few hours searching for a pocket of diamonds inside a hollow vug within a chunk of dolomite.

These crystals of quartz, a mineral that is so common it's found in virtually very class of rocks, are among the hardest and clearest found anywhere in the world. Some contain bubbles of oil or salt water and a rare few even contain a crystal within a crystal. Later, as I rode my bike outside of town, I kept looking hopefully at the road shoulder thinking I might spot one as farmers once did when plowing their fields. Double terminated crystals, according to modern day mystics, harmonize the logical with the intuitive, and the physical with the spiritual. Used to expand consciousness and share energy, they are said to store ancient wisdom and to help with life lessons, self-knowledge, centering and calming. Or perhaps they are sacred and wonderous simply because they are beautiful. Beauty, after all, has it's own power.

The river still tumbles down its rocky gorge but most of the mills are long gone. One five story stone building survives and has been made over into Canal Place. Here vendors sell antiques ranging from cream crocks and glass fly traps to old prints and farm tools and vendors peddle regional gourmet foods, 25 cent books, tee shirts and hats. A few yards away is a pedestrian bridge to Moss Island where a heap of gray stone blocks lying on the river bed is all that remains of an aqueduct that once carried the old Erie Canal across the turbulent Mohawk.

The highest single lift on the canal, 40 feet, occurs at Little Falls at lock 17. Lock 17 replaced three smaller locks and the ruins of one old structure are still visible near the present lock. Unlike most of the canal's locks the Little Falls lock has a lift type gate at its lower end, much like the guard gates you see at strategic points along the canal where protection from flooding is required.

The descent in Lock 17 is rapid enough to give the distinct sensation of a gigantic silent flush. As we dropped, dozens of tiny streams of water came squirting out from pinholes in the steel cladding of the concrete walls. We descended in a few minutes into an echoing dark slime coated chamber. At last we bottomed out, and somewhere a deep boom sounded, followed by a long groan as the massive lower gate began to ascend. Watching this 120-ton slab of steel with its massive counterweight rise slowly clear of the water to release us from the lock's dank depths was mesmerizing as was passing under its dripping mass. We were impressed with the whole 80-plus year old affair's slightly improbable looking efficiency but relieved to be free of it.

Beyond Little Falls the canal becomes increasingly scenic as it follows the Mohawk River meandering through town and country alike. At lock 12 near Schenectady stand the remains of another stone aqueduct that once carried the old canal across Schoharie Creek. Unlike the aqueduct in Little Falls at least a half dozen of the stone arches remain. Though built in the 1800s the ruins suggest far greater antiquity.

Near Schenectady the author the 1873 Harper's article described evening on the canal aboard a boat he had taken passage upon. The mule drawn boats then traveled night and day, making about the same distance *Titania* with her team of 30 Universal Motor horses did in 8 to 10 hours.

"In the evening we crossed the lower aqueduct which carries the canal over the Mohawk River and entered a dream-land of pastoral beauty. In its softness and repose it reminded us of some garden spot in England. Far and wide the acres are fertile and cultivated, the orchards are crouching in blossom, the meadows dyed with purple and white clover..." That evening plump children took the air in makeshift play pens on boat cabin roofs as a hardworking canal woman sat for a brief break in her rocking chair at the boat's stern while a young woman on another boat fed a tame robin.

Our evenings also settled into a gentle routine. Usually *Titania* tied up near sunset and her crew sat in the cockpit to make their own observations of canal life during happy hour before dinner and bedtime. In warm weather a summer evening on the canal then as now was a time of quiet beauty. We watched swallows dip a drink out of the canal and listened to frogs and singing fresh water drum thrumming in the water. A century ago travelers watched the stars and myriads of fireflies that flashed on the banks. "Each boat carries a brilliant lantern in the bow, which disperses a circle of yellow light on the watery track ahead. The tow-lines dip occasionally with a musical thrill into the water, and in advance you may hear the steady thud of the horses hoofs on the ground, or the low cry of the driver as he urges them forward..."

My own traveler's log records that after leaving Little Falls, "This was a day of winding Mohawk River, of vivid blue sky, bright green farm fields, and of turkey buzzards soaring on updrafts off hillsides. Near Fonda, the hills press in close and rail, canal, and highway squeeze together within a few hundred yards of each other. At one point they all curve around a looming steep gray rock slope some six hundred feet above. I'm steering *Titania* while a few feet above me to starboard trucks and cars stream by. As we swing around the rock outcrop, it feels like I'm driving the boat at six miles an hour down the shoulder of the Thruway. I can even read the signs- Albany 42 miles, New York City 190."

As *Titania* chugged along through the Mohawk Valley, she passed several large abandoned brick and stone factory buildings by the river. They stood silent with broken or boarded up window reflected in calm waters, reminders of an earlier time of a younger more vibrant twentieth century smokestack economy, a time when technology was analog and the Rust Belt lay far in New York's future.

Further on the canal passed through part of the old city of Schenectady, allowing me to peer up quiet residential side streets at the brick houses and exchange waves with dog walkers. Here, while I was at the tiller gazing down the side streets, I saw a dark haired young woman alone on a bench beside the canal. We looked directly at each other and I felt a thought   as if she had spoken to me- "*Where are you going aboard your boat? I want to come too...*"

Even today the quiet largely by-passed canal evokes wanderlust. Frequently as we locked through people leaned on railings beside the lock and watched. Often they asked where we were bound. A lock tender told us he wanted to step aboard one of the boats and simply go away. Perhaps part of this focused longing is prompted by the canal traveler's visibility and accessibility. As you plod along at six miles an hour, an observer or pedestrian has time to consider your passage and perhaps react to it. Modern travel now is conducted from airline terminals surrounded by vast parking lots and attempts at security with the passengers remote and invisible from casual observation. Or travel is part of the anonymous flow of thousands of speeding autos with tinted windows often obscuring the sojourners. You seldom actually see a person on an actual journey anymore in this mechanized fast moving age, except for perhaps the odd hiker or long distance cyclist peddling along the road shoulder.

Beyond the city the canal yielded in a sweeping curve to a vertical wall of solid rock about 200 feet high. Then near the dam at Cohoes the canal gradually widened. Here we passed through one of its most scenic stretches with the water studded with rocky islands, fringed with wide marshes and sometimes contained by a rugged shoreline several hundred feet high. It was as if a bit of the Maine Coast with brown water had been inserted into upstate NY. We spent our last night in the canal proper at the guard gate that protects the town of Waterford down below in the Hudson Valley from floods on the Mohawk or a mechanical failure among the staircase of five locks.

The Waterford flight, highest set of lift locks in the world, opened in 1915 and remains one of the Erie's engineering highlights. You enter through a narrow passageway cut through the dark shale of the Mohawk Valley. Then you step down five locks for a total lift of 170 feet. The lock chambers are closely spaced with no tie ups between so once you start, you're committed to finish, a process requiring about two hours. As we entered the first lock we looked out over the wide hazy blue valley below. We were about to descend to tidal water and to the sea level phase of our voyage.

Two hours later we tied up at the town's sparkling new canal visitors center and spent the night. After dinner we walked up the embankment along side the flight, peering into the canal's past for much history remains visible here. Next to lock 2 are three old stone locks dating from the mid 1800s that once connected the Erie and Champlain canals. Today they are used to control the canal water level, and especially after a rain the water roars and tumbles down them in a rushing torrent. Ferns and moss grow out of the crevices in the limestone walls, and grooves scoured by tow cables dragged over the stone ends of each lock recall a day when mules still pulled canal boats.

As we set forth on the Hudson River the next morning we entered a more dynamic and challenging world than that of the canal. Here there were tides, currents, big ships and passing tugs and barges. These along with sand bars and floating logs made watch standing slightly more critical than back in the cozy confines of the canal where I could take time to read billboards along the roadside, or peer into people's back yards and flower gardens while steering our canal packet.

The wider waters of the restless brown river lacked the intimacy of the Erie where on a quiet night tied up by a lock miles from a road bullfrogs nearby sang the summer traveler to sleep. We were eager to get on with *Titania's* cruise, to see what lay beyond the next bend and eventually to reach saltwater so we could sail again. But we looked back on our narrow waters passage where we had so often touched to past with no regrets.

Shipping News

Cement is something we take for granted. It's just sort of there in a vague all pervasive way- under our car tires, under our house, or perhaps in the case of your yacht, under her bow as a mooring block on the bottom of Fair Haven Bay. Yet modern day society would be hard pressed to exist without cement. Like steel, oil, and corn, it's a "commodity" often overlooked but utterly essential to our twenty first century way of life. Cement also sustains some of the last local Lake Ontario shipping.

These day's the lake's wide waters are mostly navigated by Sunday sailors and weekday pleasure boaters who sail in search of salmon or wind, or who simply seek to go fast and get wet. You see the occasional workboat headed to a construction site perhaps, but generally especially along the south shore of the lake, commercial enterprise is a rare sight. Many of the big ships using the Seaway pass straight through the lake well offshore and over the horizon, or they call at Canadian ports at the lake's west end, unseen by most Americans. The days when the "coal boats" moved along the shore with a smudge of trailing smoke from their stacks are only a childhood memory for most lake shore residents over fifty.

But pleasure boaters who cruise to Canada or those folks who spend any time poking around what remains of the Rochester and Oswego waterfront, have probably seen one of the last survivors of the lake's commercial fleet (though they may not remember seeing her). Little noticed and rarely commented on, she's a small gray freighter who steams around the lake delivering cement.

Her name is the *Stephen B. Roman*, and probably any yachter who has sailed the Bay of Quinte a couple of times has passed her at least once as she travels to and from the quarry just outside Picton. She is one of a small number of assorted barges and ships engaged in our last "local" cross lake trade. Others include the *English River* (another neat little gray ship who looks a lot like the *Roman*) the *Metis,* an odd barge that once was a small freighter built to fit the pre Seaway system canals of the St. Lawrence, and several barges, all Canadian vessels. Those of us who have sailed the lake for ten years or so, also remember another cement carrier the distinctive little *Day Peckinpaugh*, memorable mostly for her odd appearance.

The *Peckinpaugh* was a "canaller" whose low profile allowed her to slip under the low bridges between Oswego and her Rome NY cement terminal. She was a homely little vessel that looked sort of squashed. "You stepped DOWN two steps into her wheel house" recalled a visitor. Sometimes she went to Picton to get her cargoes herself. Sometimes she got her cement from the *Roman*. I saw her several times on the wall in Oswego or along side the *Roman* getting filled up, and once or twice I spotted her out on the open lake. Once I paused briefly to compliment a man on her deck in Oswego on the pretty flower boxes on her stern. He told me the old veteran had an interesting history, that she had been a small tanker on salt water and that she had been hard at work since 1921. As of this writing she was laid up in Erie Pennsylvania awaiting an uncertain fate, but Lake Ontario's other cement carriers continue to run their regular delivery routes competing successfully with trains and trucks even in this day of federal highway trust funds and cheap diesel fuel.

One day while in Oswego as a tourist to see a visiting tall ship, I looked over at the Essroc terminal where the *Stephen B. Roman* ties up every week and thought-how odd. Here's a ship that comes in here all the time with a cargo absolutely essential to our daily lives and yet most people don't even know her name. I walked into the office of the terminal and a friendly young man took a moment off from watching his digital scale read outs as he loaded a truck with powdered cement to give me the ship's phone number and I made a couple of calls. "Come on up for lunch" said a cheery Canadian accent, presumably belonging to one of the mates. "The Captain will be here then". And so on a blustery fall day I did so, and over homemade cream of celery soup and a western sandwich and fresh pot of coffee I learned a little about the most familiar "cement boat" on Lake Ontario from her Captain, Dan Bielby.

Captain Dan, a life long Great Lakes mariner began his shipping career straight out of high school. He worked his way up through the ranks in the time honored fashion of merchant mariners on the lakes, and served as the *Roman*'s second mate before becoming captain of another carrier. He rejoined the ship fourteen years ago and has been with her since. He graciously assured me he had plenty of time for questions as the vessel would be unloading until after dark and all he had on his schedule that afternoon was a quick trip to Walmart.

The *Stephen B.Roman* is currently owned by the ESSROC/Italcementi, a big international outfit that operates quarries all over the world. Their Picton quarry, one of the biggest on the lakes, produces about 790,000 tons of cement a year and about 200 people work there blasting, crushing and "cooking" the clinkers into powdered Portland cement. As ships go, the *Stephen B. Roman* is a rather good looking vessel. She's 488 feet long, considerably smaller than the long low 700 plus foot long "lakers" that were built as bulk carriers to haul pelletized hematite ore, grain, or steel slag, and unlike modern day ships with their stark angularity and slab sidedness she has a little "style" to her lines. As long as I've known her, she's always been cement colored with white upper works. She retains the rounded shape and raked bow of an older generation of freighters. Her wheel house and stern are pleasingly curved and she always looks tidy and trim to me when I see her pass by on the lake or Bay of Quinte, unlike the often rust stained, dented, and battered looking salties and bigger lakers who go down to salt water on the Seaway.

Her crew works pretty hard to keep her looking that way I suspect. On the day of our visit, there was lots of fresh gray deck paint to avoid underfoot, and I saw scarcely a speck of rust anywhere on a ship nearing her fortieth birthday.

The *Roman* was built in Lauzon Quebec in 1965 and began life as the *Fort William* as part of the Canada Steamship Lines. She has three holds and is powered by four Fair Banks Morse diesels that generate about 6600 horsepower. She draws 35 feet and carries 7000 metric tons of cement when full. But back when she was first launched, she was a package freighter, that is, a small coastal trader carrying general cargo around the great lakes. She transported rolled steel from Hamilton, deck cargoes, school buses to Thunder Bay, pickles and just about anything else "that could be put on a pallet and moved with a fork lift" explained her captain. She had sliding hatches on deck and a sort of big elevator to move the freight up from the hold.

She got off to a rough start too. In her first year of service in September she capsized in Montreal Harbor. Improperly loaded with too much deck cargo up high and not enough yet in her hold for stability she took on a twenty degree list. That in itself probably wouldn't have done her in, but unfortunately during the loading process a series of side hull ports and hatches had been left open. As she listed the water came pouring in and the *Fort Williams* swamped and rolled over. Thanks to a combination of bad moves five people died. The *Fort Williams* was pumped out and put back together and went off to work for another ten years.

As a package freighter she was designed to compete with trucks and trains and was capable of a fairly brisk seventeen knot speed. But she wasn't fast enough. Trucks and trains also didn't have to contend with the occasional day of fifteen foot waves that could shift cargoes and when the occasional pallet of merchandise slid around in that steel hold, it sometimes ended up on the "bump and scratch" discount table. Easy to see why containerized cargo on huge ships got to be so popular. The less efficient package freight business died in the late 1970s, and the *Fort William* was laid up for lack of work. Around 1982 she was towed up to Collingwood for a major re-fit. She was totally gutted and turned into a bulk carrier.

Intrigued about the process of moving cement around, I asked the captain just how do you do it? He explained that powdered dry cement can be moved around if it's "fluidized" by the addition of air. Lots of it. The *Roman* carries six large air compressors to push the powder around. The three cargo holds have sloped bottoms, just like the farmer's hopper bottom grain wagon and a huge pump at the bottom of each hold moves the stuff through a series of pipes and through a large tunnel in the bottom of the ship. An elaborate system of plumbing and over a hundred electrically driven stops or gates direct the flow to two black discharge hoses that carry it up to the storage elevators on shore. "We can move 300 tons an hour here. In Cleveland where the terminal has three hoses, we can unload 500 tons an hour." The entire system is sealed- with nothing more than the rare a puff of dust to reveal it's at work and much of the noise from it is directed inward to make the process as palatable as possible to the ship's near neighbors when she's in port. The ship carries a larger than usual complement of engineers in order to keep the complex cargo handling system operating smoothly. Time is after all money, in shipping as elsewhere and production is the name of the game.

So what happens if you spring a leak I asked? Captain Dan laughed "It's not pretty" he said, adding that one of the lake's cement carriers during a period of winter lay up apparently had a leaky hatch. "There were a couple lumps the size of school buses down there". The *Roman* herself once suffered from a very small leak- apparently just a single bolt hole."There was a lump the size of a Volkswagon down there. We had to chip it out and carry it up in buckets."

I learned that the ship always loads her cement at the Picton quarry and she follows a regular delivery route. She runs to Oswego and Rochester, often with a "split load" and then goes back to Picton for another load. This then goes to Toronto or perhaps out to Cleveland, and, at least formerly, to Detroit's bleak Rouge River area waterfront. It takes her a couple of days to make her Lake Ontario runs. At 300 tons an hour unloading rate, she is often in and out of Oswego in less than 24 hours. Her Captain typically works two months on and then is off for a month while the relief captain takes over. The hourly wage crew may work more days afloat.

The ship has a crew of 18 including deckhands, engine room staff, and mates, many of whom reside near the St. Catherines area by the Welland Canal. Sometimes while the vessel is in transit between locks, they are able to slip home for a quick visit with the family. In port the crew has to monitor and direct the loading and unloading as well as take care of any number of odd jobs, while Captain Dan in Oswego and Rochester, at least, has to deal with customs and their eleven pages of paperwork for him on every trip. (In an ironic note on the state of maritime commerce in the late twentieth century the customs men drive up to the ship from either the Syracuse or Rochester's airport). Then there's always painting.

The *Roman* owes her job to a quirk of geology that left the north shore of the lake with extensive outcrops of limestone that gave rise to most of Ontario Province's 500 million dollar a year cement industry. There are several quarries along the lakeshore besides the one at Picton, one of the largest on the lake. Underneath Lake Ontario layers of sedimentary rock tilt slightly north-south. Along the south shore the top layer consists of sedimentary sandstone, with the older deposits of limestone under that. But the limestone angles upward and reaches the surface on the lake's north shore, giving rise to the strange flat mesa like shape of Dry Hill by Watertown and the low lying level plains of Point Traverse, Main Duck, Galloo, and Stony Islands. One of the layers of limestone, originally laid down in a clear shallow sunlit tropical sea 500 million years ago, often contains fossils including trilobites. So the stylized spiral ammonite shell corporate emblem on the *Roman's* stack is quite appropriate.

As we talked in the wardroom over our coffee a crewman came in and asked with a grin "Anyone want a boat? Look out the window". We peered out a nearby porthole to see a small unmanned orange and white runabout gently drifting down the river headed out to sea. Someone's boat had come untied. This prompted a round of speculation about "salvage" (the Coast Guard had already been notified though) and then recollections about other rescues at sea.

The *Stephen B. Roman* has lent aid to several misguided mariners over the years that were "lost" out on the lake back in the days before inexpensive GPS technology was so prevalent. One hapless sailboat skipper and crew had been traveling in circles for about 36 hours off Rochester before he got guidance on where to go. Perhaps most amusing to Captain Dan was their request for a drink of fresh water, even as they floated on a 600 foot deep sea of the stuff.

On another occasion the lookout noticed two men on a jet ski about five miles offshore near Sodus Bay. They had presumably come over to jump the ship's wake a few times and the watch stander noted that "One guy was paddling the thing with a little plastic paddle." It was late in the day, the sun was getting low and the land lay dim on the distant horizon. So the *Stephen B. Roman* turned around and went back to check on them- out of gas. The Jet Ski owner had been demonstrating his craft to a perspective buyer and had zipped offshore "without even a towel" to ward off the wet. With night's chill coming on, the castaways were very happy to accept a little gas from the ship's supply for its outboard inflatable.

"We got the Zodiac a few years ago when we converted over to the canopy type life rafts," said the Captain. The former lifeboats (one of which is now on exhibit at the Oswego H. Lee White Marine Museum) were far too cumbersome and slow to launch. The Zodiac he explained would take the rafts in tow to clear the ship should they ever be launched and also can be put over the side quickly for man overboard recovery. In drills "We can turn the ship in a Williamson turn and get back to the object in the water, launch the Zodiac and make the recovery in nine minutes" noted Captain Dan. He added after a brief pause "I wish we had had that Zodiac back when that barge went down."

He was referring to a tragedy that was played out upon the lake's unforgiving waters back in 1993. On a November night the *Stephen B. Roman* responded to the sinking of a barge but was unable to get a lifeboat launched fast enough to save the two men that were aboard. I remembered the incident vaguely and also recalled rowing the dinghy on a quiet September evening a few years ago over to a derelict wooden barge stranded in the shallows of Chaumont Bay a little northeast of the Isthmus. We floated around inside the hulk wondering how it had gotten there. The ruin retained some of the furnishings and structures of its restaurant days. It had been a strangely melancholy and slightly mysterious relic with the bar stools and some of the fixtures still in place as we could see when we paddled around among the massive rotting timbers and peered up through the holes in the deck. "Was that the leaky old wooden restaurant barge they were trying to get across the lake?" I asked. He nodded and recalled they never should have been out there. The captain of the tug got a year for negligent homicide.

The facts of the tragedy were this according to legal docket 96-1484 obtained off the Internet.

During the fall of 1993 one captain McHugh of J&M Marine Towing was asked to transport two old wooden barges across the lake. These had sat on the bottom in shallow water on Chaumont Bay for many years and had been used there as a restaurant and bar. A Syracuse based businessman sought to transport them across to Onondaga Lake. The water logged wooden hulks were not in good shape and needed constant pumping just to keep them afloat. So two men were stationed on board to keep several gasoline-powered pumps running. A marine surveyor examined the hulks and told the tug captain the only way he could expect to get them across the lake was to tow slow and to pick a day of "ideal weather conditions that should include winds less than ten knots and waves less than two feet."

The morning of November 25 the tug captain and crew attempted to make the crossing with both barges in tow. I remember it as being a breezy mild late November day with winds considerably more than ten knots, and the court docket states there were six to eight foot seas rolling in at the lake's northeastern corner. Hardly the conditions recommended. One account of the tragedy says the tow ran aground. Another says the line between the barges broke. Possibly both are correct. At any rate, the *CL No. 1* turned back and left one barge in the bay (where we saw it a couple years later). She made a late start the next day, now with only the smaller barge in tow.

According to the court docket Captain McHugh failed to check his ship's VHF for the continuous weather broadcasts from the U.S. and Canada.

As it happened, for over an hour before the tow left from the bay at dusk on November 26, both weather services were broadcasting gale warnings with southeast winds building to 35 knots and waves that night four to six feet building to five to eight feet the next day. As the legal document goes on in its dry language "While these predicted wind and wave conditions were given continuously by both weather services defendant acknowledges he never listened to them."

As the tow entered the lake, the *CL No. 1* and her barge headed almost directly into the waves with a strengthening south wind and short steep seas now building quickly. The waves began washing right over the old hulk's bow and sides astern and the tug crew saw the generator powered running lights go out. Perhaps some or all of the pump engines failed too sometime during the night. As *CL No. 1* and her increasingly water logged tow crawled slowly towards the sheltering lee of the lake's south shore and were perhaps within sight of the city lights and the harbor's red flashing lighthouse beacon, things got worse. The tug crew saw a man waving a flashlight on board, then at about 2 am the barge began to break up. Despite being just six miles offshore, it was still rough for the strong southeaster had rolled up six to eight footers so the barge went down fast. The *CL No.1* radioed a mayday and one man on the barge was seen jumping overboard with a life preserver. The tug then tried to turn back to rescue the man in the water only to foul her towline on her prop. Now helpless she was adrift and unable to reach the man struggling in the bitterly cold black wind swept lake.

Several vessels and the U.S. and Canadian Coast Guard responded to the mayday. One of those ships was the *Stephen B. Roman*. Though her crew was unable to recover either of the barge's lost men the ship did stand by and eventually took the tug in tow after its crew managed to cut through the cable between the snarl on the prop and the barge. If they hadn't gotten free of the sunken barge it was quite possible in the heavy seas that they would have had their shaft pulled out and the tug would then also have sunk with more men swimming in 45 degree water in the dark. Sadly when the Coast Guard team pulled the crew member from the water he still had a weak pulse but he did not survive. "His death" notes docket 96-1484 "was determined to be the result of drowning." Captain Dan remembered "They never did find the second body". The next year the *Stephen B. Roman* received an update in life saving equipment in the form of new rafts and the high speed Zodiac inflatable.

The lake can be an unfriendly place in the fall and winter even for a 488 foot 7000 ton freighter. Asked about storms Bielby said he had videotaped eighteen foot waves on the lake. The ship's relief captain once made a run from Oswego to Rochester during which the crew estimated they had 22 foot waves to contend with, big enough to cause minor damage to the vessel's forward bulwarks. The *Roman,* while sizeable and sturdy, is not invincible notes her captain. Respect for the lake is always in order.

The ship usually gets laid up in Toronto for the winter though as an experiment the company decided to try extending her season into January last year. It was a good old fashioned winter with lots of ice. Up in the Bay of Quinte by the quarry the ice was eighteen inches thick. And the turning basin in the Genesee River froze over, something it rarely does. Normally the ship takes about ten minutes to turn around here, with about forty feet to spare on either end. But with the ice cover last winter it took her over two hours. "She goes through ice pretty well, but not sideways".

Although the ship makes her regular delivery run year in and year out, entering Oswego and Rochester dozens of times each season, the trips are far from routine. One feature of the Genesee River that makes life interesting for her crew is its ancient Stutson Street drawbridge, slated for replacement in the near future. "It's in terrible shape". "We're the only vessel it has to open 100 per cent for regularly" and sometimes it appears to be a struggle and chunks of the bridge have fallen on the deck. The ship's crew apparently doesn't take bridge opening totally for granted, approaching it each time with a healthy skepticism. Even so, once the relief captain got caught short when the bridge didn't lift. He drifted over onto the east side of the river where a forty foot yacht, the *"Never Again Two"* was tied up at Shumways. It got a little bit squashed as Captain Dan put it. "It didn't look too bad on the outside. But the bulkheads and the interior were sort of skewed. The insurance totaled it. *Never Again III.* ".

The bridge not withstanding, the *Roman's* captain enjoys the wooded park like atmosphere of the Genesee and the protection of its scenic deep gorge. People walk by the ship with their dogs, and deer ignore "that big gray thing" and stroll down to the water for a drink. A recent photo taken with a digital camera with regular lens on the wheel house bulkhead showed a young buck in velvet peering in a window-he couldn't' have been over twenty feet away. For the *Roman*, the Genesee River is presumably a secluded little gunkhole much like Main Duck's inner harbor is to our 32 foot yacht.

After patiently and cheerfully answering my questions Captain Dan asked if we'd like a tour. We enthusiastically said yes please and followed him down into the engineering area where we could peek into the sound proofed control area and look down through the grating at the tops of the four main engines and other machinery. Although the ship can do seventeen knots, she often steams with just two engines at a slower speed to save fuel. She carries two hundred tons and usually goes through about eleven tons a day.

Aft we inspected the hydraulic rams that operate the rudder along with the machinery for emergency steering. Everything we examined was spotless and I recalled the Captain's earlier remarks abut the ship's general condition. She had recently been in dry dock for a round of extensive inspections as mandated by the Coast Guard, and underwriters. The fastest you can ever get through it is five days and that's how long she took. Some ships receive quantities of new steel in repairs that are measured in tons. For the *Roman's* last inspection, it took a few pounds of steel to fix her up. One reason she is in such good shape is that she has spent her entire life on fresh water. She's never been below Montreal.

We hiked up to the wheelhouse to inspect the state of the art navigational gear and to look out over the deck and the harbor. Seeing the ship extending far out before me, I viewed Oswego with a new perspective. It looked way smaller than at the helm of our sailboat. The place looked downright cozy for maneuvering a 400 plus foot ship without any tug assistance. After the wheelhouse we stopped in to check out the captain's modest but comfortable quarters complete with Lazy-Boy chair and screwed down computer, the screen reflecting the latest round with customs- ah yes, my "tasks" said the skipper with a wry smile. "I spend a lot of time on paperwork".

Our tour through the narrow corridors of painted steel and gray linoleum, in and out of odd shaped rooms with slanting floors, and up and down steep narrow steel ladders, brought back memories of my several brief student voyages aboard fishery research vessels to Georges Bank and the Nova Scotia area back in the late 1970's. Alas, when I asked if the *Roman* ever took anyone on junkets, I learned her former guest cabin had been eliminated to give one of the mates more room.

After spending over two hours enjoying the ship's hospitality we reluctantly departed, climbing down the ladder back to the dock. After we drove home, the crew presumably checked their computer readouts and the ship's draft marks to make the final tally of cement and then cast off for the Rochester run steaming into the night with yet another load of footers, foundations, abutments, and the like for central New York.

After fourteen years on her bridge, Captain Dan seems quite content to keep quietly and reliably delivering a commodity that we can't do without. He assured me assuming the present economic situation continues, that the ship and her Canadian crew will probably be a part of our maritime scene on the lake for some time to come-earning an honest dollar afloat, one of the very few vessels left on the lake still able to do so.

Back in 1930 marine historian George Cuthbertson wrote in his book *Freshwater* of the twentieth century Great Lakes package freighter "Sturdy, dependable and patient, these efficient ships are the very essence of freshwater transportation. Neglected by marine artists and often dismissed as unsightly craft the Great Lakes package freighter has strength and dignity..." So remember that heritage the next time you see the *English River* or the *Stephen B. Roman* in their present day incarnation.

An Island Passage

Four days after the shortest night of the year a solitary yacht sailed slowly down the lake. As twilight slowly deepened to darkness, the white sloop slipped along on a broad reach over the calm water, distant freighter lights twinkling to the south from a procession of lakers entering and parting the Welland Canal. As the first stars appeared overhead sounds began to dominate the watch stander's senses. Even as vision paled, hearing sharpened.

A gull resting for the night upon the water and startled by the passing yacht cried out with a piercing sorrowful voice as the bow wave whispered and sighed like wind in distant trees. A ship several miles away passed by, and the deep muffled thump of its engine carried on the wind to the watch stander. The breeze strengthened after sunset, and the yacht, now sailing near six knots, began to roll to the small swells passing under her. Her forefoot pushed up the water before her with the sound of gentle surf, surging, swishing, and gushing. In the darkness, the leech of the unseen genoa vibrated with a low pitched flutter as the yacht rolled and a topping lift fitting squeaked quietly as the wires inside the aluminum mast clanked and rattled. Below decks the constant soft sibilance of running water flowing past the yacht's hull sounded like a gentle summer stream.

Not until well after 11 pm did the last western glow of dusk merge with the lights of Toronto astern. Here and there other lesser glows on the horizon marked the locations of Niagara Falls, Oshawa and Rochester.

This passage had begun in the morning at a speed of two knots over a glassy lake with the yacht creating a train of tiny ripples and with just the slightest whisper of a bow wave. In the hot June morning the passage had seemed almost dreamlike as the boat ghosted over the flat water. With an almost imperceptible zephyr of wind the boat moved at three knots. Though the crew could barely feel the wind on their faces, it moved the yacht's 9000 pounds eastward at walking speed.

Now, as darkness gathered, the yacht loafed along with a light helm swinging a bit to the passing swells while slowly the stars moved over the night's vault. A satellite crawled across the heavens and the milky way's arch rose out of the east after midnight. Once a greenish streak of a meteor shot straight downward off the bow. A few hours after the sleepy watch stander had gone to her bunk, a last quarter moon rose mellow and golden over the starboard bow.

After I had gone to bed I lay in my bunk and listened to the rumble and surge of the bow wave a few feet from my ear and wondered what songs does *Titania* sing as she sails? Does she murmur and sigh over past anchorages and good friends met there, now gone these 35 years since her first cruise? Does she recall old salts who once sat in her cockpit talking and laughing of other night passages or day sails? I suspect she sings of blue skies, soft winds and clear sunlit waters rippling over the limestone ledges of Canada's shoreline. I think she whispers about still nights anchored under the stars in a quiet cove where on shore fireflies twinkled among the grass. She remembers and sings of long easy days filled with light and warmth, for like the butterflies and flowers of the country roadside, she's a creature of summer.

Perhaps some of her memories involved the destination that had just slipped astern, that of Canada's largest city Toronto. In her younger days, our boat had been owned by a Rochester Yacht Club member who had perhaps sailed her down to the city to call at other yacht clubs and to linger among the city's park islands where we had just spent three days.

New York City has its central park, San Diego has Balboa and its museums and Toronto has its park islands. City parks, where people gather to picnic play and seek a bit of space, are part of the heart and soul of the city. Toronto's islands are a priceless asset. And like many a city park used and owned by hundreds of thousands of people, they have also sparked intense passions and debates through the years. There is something about islands that makes them special and Torontonians have treasured theirs from the start.

Toronto's park was once a protective sand spit that curved around the city's harbor like a miniature Cape Cod or Sandy Hook. Then a huge storm broke through the narrow neck of the spit and cut it off from the mainland. The cut was stabilized and deepened to become the eastern gap and over the years the sheltering marsh and sand bars of the barrier were transformed into a island archipelago with dredged deepened lagoons.

Once a windswept haunt for fishermen and squatters and a small military outpost, by the 1820s the islands had already become a popular summer spot for the town of York. The low-lying shifting often flooded land was too ephemeral for easy ownership and its marshes with attendant "agues and intermittent fevers" (malaria) also deterred permanent settlement. Yet then as now there was an irresistible appeal about a low lying land surrounded by water. The islands seemed far more remote than they really were, and city dwellers loved their spaces and long empty shorelines. Soon hotels, summer tents, and cottages came to its sandy shores, and before long the city had appropriated much of the area and was leasing out lots to homebuilders and tenters with a formal city park being laid out starting around 1880.

A few hardy summer people liked the place enough to establish permanent settlements. For over a century, though, a constant tension has pushed and pulled at the islands. Should anyone be allowed to live here? Should the airport be expanded? Should it become an expanse of close clipped lawn belonging only to transient day visitors? Should a bridge be built and the road be widened and more parking installed? With so many "stakeholders" a commons belonging to everyone prompts a multiplicity of views and hot exchanges between passionate users. A few months after *Titania's* visit, the mayoral election in Toronto featured the future of the park islands as a central campaign theme.

Today, the one time sand spit is continually added onto at its east end by humans. As we chugged into the harbor, a procession of dump trucks loaded with rubble paraded down the long narrow eastern spit in the distance like ants bearing grains of sand to continue its slow accretion out into the lake. The eastern spit is so new and raw a land that little lives here save for thousands of nesting gulls and cormorants and a few pioneering cottonwoods, willows and shrubs.

The eastern spit is accessible from the mainland and harbors several large marinas and boat yards reached by a bicycle and jogging trail that we explored aboard our trusty two wheelers one evening. This trail was far less populated than the path to the city's west where a veritable sea of roller bladders, joggers, walkers, pram pushers and cyclists made an evening ride hectic with a mob of non motorized traffic flowing past the slow moving sight seeing cyclist. Here, though, giant cottonwoods spread their canopies over an empty path and we could poke along and gaze upon tall reeds, grasses and summer wild flowers bending to the lake breeze on either side.

Being boaters we naturally peddled out to inspect the marinas and found ourselves in that emptiest of coastal landscapes, a boat yard during high summer. Here a few yachts squatted on the hard packed fill propped by jack stands to await refits, surveys, or changes in ownership. We paused to gaze upon a husky ferro-cement hull, freshly painted in bright white. Rigging stained with the rust of saltwater, anchors, chains, and an assortment of boat parts lay scattered on the sun baked ground nearby. This vessel's refit was progressing. She would perhaps, like a spawning Lake Ontario eel, someday return to the sea.

Other nearby hulls were clearly less fortunate. In the boat yard of mid-summer, hope and anticipation rest alongside disillusionment and despair. In few other places do life's varied outcomes sit so starkly exposed out in the open for all to examine and scrutinize. We lingered by the ferro hull, obviously still a going enterprise. What clear tropical waters had passed under her home built keel and when had warm trade winds last whistled through her shrouds?

I climbed up to peer into a nearby wooden hull, once graceful and strong gleaming with varnish and fresh paint, but now only a dried mummified shell, a gray husk of a yacht. Where were the family members and friends that had lounged in her cockpit? How many children now grown and gone had held onto that tiller? This biodegradable boat stripped of fittings and gear was well on her way to becoming one with the elements again.

We spent several days among the park islands tied up at a popular municipal docking area at Hanlans Point, hard by the ferry dock and the proposed bridge link and airport that was sparking such fierce controversy among the picnickers, bridge building contractors, Bombadier aircraft factory union workers, ferry boat crews and other stakeholders. Watching the small noisy airplanes swoop down low over our mast as we chugged into the channel by the point, our vote was with the ferry boat crews and no more pavement and cars contingent.

Once the boat was settled we enjoyed peddling about for with their level paved trails and leashed dogs and lack of cars the islands were a bicycle paradise. Then we would return to sit on the boat and watch the daily routine of a great city park unfold before us.

As the first ferries docked and disgorged their cargoes, the resident Canada geese flocks that graze each morning upon the short clipped lawn took to the waters to paddle around in the lagoons dodging the frequent male mute swans also out on patrol. Most of the dumpy short necked brown and gray night herons had also forsaken the shorelines to hide out in the wilder shadier areas of the archipelago by mid morning. But the gulls were made of sterner stuff. They stood guard over favored trash cans and picnic tables shrieking at and chasing off any other bird that dared to approach their treasure.

As the day moved on crowds of Torontonians seeking respite from concrete and asphalt thickened. Many park users were of eastern or Indian origin. Bearded men with turbans, and slight dusky women wearing long colorful saris mingled with long legged blonds and athletic men sporting rings and pins embedded in various unlikely parts of their torsos and faces. All day the boaters kept coming in to the tie ups along the municipal marina and by mid afternoon no empty spots remained. Dogs on shore leave frisked about in loose packs, boaters headed to the nearest barbecue to fire up for dinner and the folding chairs were deployed on shore. A beautifully restored wooden Chris Craft the *Incomprehensible* tied up astern of our Chris Craft sailboat. Her friendly crew told us to be sure to stay for the fireworks competition. So we did.

With the evening came a veritable parade of excursion boats processing slowly down the narrow channel past our yacht. We stared at the passengers a few yards away and some of them stared at us. The *Island Queen*, The *Wayward Princess*, The *Maple Leaf*, The *Spirit of Toronto*, The *Oriole* all slipped by- dinner boats of widely varied shape and size and design ranging from the basic slab sided sixty foot box whose sound system speakers were lashed with twine to the canvas canopy over her steel deck to the elegant snow white mini-cruise ships with uniformed crew. As darkness fell, the dinner boat sound systems got louder and louder with the sound of their bass sometimes carrying a mile or more over the open water.

The decision to stay another day for fireworks was easy. Already island indolence was taking hold. We would make up the time with a straight through passage down the lake to head home we figured. So the next morning we rode our bikes over to the part of the archipelago where a stubborn small outpost of islanders still resides year around in their eclectic little cottages. Somehow the Ward Islanders have resisted the burning and bulldozing pressures that for the last fifty years have been at work transforming most of the summer tent cities and cottages into grass. Today their small cabins and huts stand under shady trees a few feet apart surrounded by neatly kept mini gardens and postage stamp yards often fenced and walled. The walkways and "streets" between them are just big enough for a bicycle and we found this tranquil car-free community tucked way on the doorstep of big busy Toronto utterly enchanting.

Thanks to their tenuous hold here on leases and lots subject to non-renewal by the municipality, no one had torn his turn of the century cottage down and replaced it with a glitzy 4000 foot mini-mansion. This unnatural suppression of the relentless bigger is better to build by the water urge has left an enclave frozen in architectural time, charming and immensely appealing in its slightly ramshackle eccentricity. The scale of the little homes was completely appropriate to the scale of the small land upon which they were built. I, who mostly landscape by letting the poison ivy grow as ground cover in the corners of my yard, marveled at the ingenuity and sophistication of their landscaping. Now as I sailed along through the night, I pondered the timeless appeal of islands as places to live or visit and their particular fascination for those of us who travel with boats.

Dawn was lightening the eastern sky by 4 am and the horizon was clearly visible when I came back on deck after my four hours off. We were now over eighty miles from our start point at Port Dalhousie, two thirds of the way down the lake making good time with such light wind. By 9 am Main Duck Island, our next destination was just nineteen miles ahead.

Sometimes the island appears in clear weather as a series of small dark dots that rise above a sharp edged horizon and then coalesce into a low solid line of tree tops joined by land. And other times, as happened on this morning, the low lying land simply solidifies out of the haze about five miles away as a faint blue smudge in front of the boat. Always I feel a little lift of joy when I first sight it. To me Main Duck has always seemed like a sort of Brigadoon, a slightly magical place that exists just for one fair summer day before it vanishes astern and disappears again from my world. This summer we had picked nearly the longest day of the year to visit and linger by its pebble beaches and to walk its shoreline ledges.

I have visited this place dozens of times since *Ariel* and I first voyaged here in 1980. I never tire of the place and always leave it with regret. Yet when I try to describe it to a landlubber I have difficulty capturing its essence and fall back on clichés like "it's just a neat place". There is really very little here. Perhaps that is much of its appeal.

Main Duck lies about 20 miles south of Kingston and about ten miles east of Prince Edward County's long out thrust arm of Point Traverse. It mostly consists of stone. When the glaciers spread south they scraped the layers of limestone here clean of soil, leaving bedrock and a few pockets of thin earth behind. The entire island is tilted gently north-south reflecting the general lay of the land in the lake's northeastern corner. The geologists refer to this slant as "regional dip" and Galloo, Grenadier, and Stony Island and Point Peninsula and other lake headlands all display the precise same tilt. Main Duck tapers off underwater on its south side at the same angle so you can wade many yards out and still be in waist deep water. Even a half-mile offshore, shoals reach out to threaten the unwary vessel that cuts the corner here.

But on its north side the outcrop of rock that forms the island drops away sharply in a nearly vertical underwater cliff. You can sail around its bold high point close inshore with eighty feet on the fathometer. The island's north side is also quite irregular with several large coves that make fine deepwater anchorages in calm weather. This asymmetry lends to the hint of mystery about Main Duck. It's different from the other islands in this part of the lake. Galloo, Stony, Little Galloo all line up with longer axis running northeast southwest and have smooth coasts with little in the way of protected anchorages to welcome the overnighter. Not so pork chop shaped Main Duck.

But none of these coves is a good all weather anchorage. When the wind goes north you find yourself on a lee shore and more than one yacht has ended up in a situation like the hapless little coal carrier *John Randall* whose bones are still visible lying in a few feet of water in the largest island cove. Main Duck does offer one inside all weather harbor. (Perhaps that's why it's the Main Duck as opposed to the near by False Ducks and Ducklings.) Once past its narrow entrance, your yacht lies within a completely sheltered little pond fringed by cattail and with a soft mud bottom. A narrow strip of gravel separates this tranquil marshy little backwater from the windswept open lake. Here even deep draft *Titania* can consort with muskrats and snapping turtles while a boat length away bullfrogs bellow from shore and a blue heron stalks his dinner.

We eased *Titania* into the little harbor on June 25 and anchored by gently shoving her keel into the mud and then dropping the hook. We then decided to go for a hike, a timeless pleasure here, and once ashore found the landscape unusually lush and green, thanks to abundant rains. Spring lingers here on a small island surrounded by cool lake waters. The lilacs were still in bloom along the shore where once a fisherman's cottage had stood. We set off down the foot path that less than twenty years ago was a road around the little anchorage. Before us a carpet of grayish green drought tolerant cinquefoil grew in the compacted thin soil of the former roadbed. The flowers were all open for the morning sun and the cheerful glow of gold outlined a yellow flower road before us. Further on giant white hogweed flowers loomed over the grass and vegetation. Their saucer like shapes floating over the land looked a bit like distant UFO's. How had the hogweed seeds traveled over 12 or more miles of open water to reach the island? Had they floated like mangrove sprouts or did they fly on a gale to the island?

June is the time of reptile passions and on the stone walls of the old roofless structure by the dock we found a pair of garter snakes cuddled up in each corner of the ruins. Their coils and curves draped over one another in a careless easy sensuality. Their two heads were up side by side as they eyed us warily. Their stripes glowed as bright as butter. In the east facing side of the end wall, we spotted several more single snakes lying in sunlit crevices and crannies. They were warming up after a chilly night before they slid off into the grass to hunt whatever little snakes eat for dinner.

Wherever we went that day we kept running across turtles looking for nesting sites. Mostly painted turtles and snappers, they were on beaches, in cleared grassy areas, by the path and along the shore. Frequent areas of scratched up earth appeared to be aborted nest attempts and several times we detoured around turtles laying eggs. As we picked our way through the tall grass at the end of the harbor, ever alert for stepping on a snake or turtle, surf murmured on the gray shingle shore a few yards away and a cool breeze moved over the land. Now and then a bull frog held forth and I paused to listen to the stillness surrounding us.

Mixed in with the murmur of the surf I kept hearing faint plaintive cries, keenings and what sounded like distant shouts. I suppose it was only the voices of gulls, but I kept wondering about the shipwrecks around the island and the lost rum runners, fishermen, and mariners, cast away on these ledges during storms calling for help with no one to hear them.

Part of the appeal of Main Duck for me, is the ease with which the amateur naturalist can observe wildlife here. While only the toughest and most tolerant creatures can co-exist with the humans on Toronto's islands, here wild creatures live in a lightly used land (at least early in the summer before bass season opens). Perhaps like the Galapagos, wildlife here shows a charming innocence as to how dangerous humans are. A snake will lie on the dock right beside you if you keep still, and the snapping turtles will swim right up to the boat to check out that interesting smell coming from the sink drain after you drain tuna juice off the can. I once stood on the dock and watched a fish go to sleep. I'd never seen a fish take a nap before. The ten inch small mouth bass swam slowly out from under the dock into the open water shallows of the anchorage and then settled into the soft gray silt looking just like a dog flopping down into a comfy bed. It worked out a little hollow in the mud and then was very still. I'm sure it was taking a snooze.

Later that day we watched a loon fishing in the anchorage diving and coming up a few yards from *Titania,* ignoring us as it went about its business of finding dinner for itself and its youngsters. And another time while sitting on the dock I saw a muskrat swim under the structure with a mouthful of vegetation. Peering between the boards I watched as the baby about 4 inches long swam to meet its parent for mealtime directly beneath where I lay. There is probably no other freshwater mammal cuter than a baby muskrat viewed from a foot away.

The mile and a half hike out to the lighthouse takes you past a curious landscape. The nearly flat low lying island's thin soil and frequent large areas of bare bedrock don't lend themselves to rapid re-vegetation. Once mostly forested, later grazed, large areas remain tree free after being fallow for many years. Today they form little savannahs of prairie like grass. These "barrens" are similar to larger mainland areas where unique and globally rare plants and insects are known to reside. The trees that do grow often seem to sprout right from stone. There are few traces of the island's century long human habitation in the island's interior, a few bits of rusty machinery and the rutted road worn down to bedrock by the light house keeper's truck being the only obvious signs of usage. But the island has long been a place of keen interest to humans. Undoubtedly, it was used by the Indians as a fishing outpost and stop-over while later settlers farmed and grazed it. Two of the best known island owners were Claude Cole and John Foster Dulles.

The earlier of these known widely as King Cole, was a colorful strong willed overlord who lived on Main Duck for thirty years in the summer. He leased the land around the small harbor to a dozen or so fishermen and a number of them worked and lived here with their families during the warmer months netting lake trout and whitefish. Old photos show their camps and net reels along the shores flanking the approach to the little inner anchorage.

A newspaper account states that Cole went first to the islands as a hired gun, given the task of clearing the island of wild cattle left by a previous settler. He took his sailing skiff and rifle over and did the job, but then decided to stay and try his hand there at farming. After several years he purchased the island outright for 1200 dollars and experimented with race horses, cattle, and buffalo. His main profits came from his fishing rights though he is also said to have been in sympathy with the bootleggers who used Main Duck as a stopover. He ran a husky wooden fish tug back and forth between Cape Vincent and the island and, says historian Willis Metcalfe, his wife Annie was an able helmsman as well, often taking the tug with its load of fresh fish into Cape Vincent.

The Coles wintered on the island a few times and in later years left the farm in the care of their son Cecil, his wife Edna, and various other companions. Besides looking after the stock the caretakers also cut and stored ice for next summer's fishing season. In the winter the only means of communication between the isolated island and the outside world was by letters sent over to the mainland on small rafts equipped with evergreen branches for sails. A February 9 1933 item in the Watertown area paper reported on word received from the island by Mr. And Mrs. Cole. It read in part;
Dear Father and Mother, The wind is down the lake and blowing hard so we are sending a raft and hope someone will find it soon. We had a fine run up and found everything fine here. There is just a little ice in the upper end of the pond. Cecil ran the tug up in the mud and has her engine nearly laid up for winter. Clifford had everything in good order... We had heavy wind, rain and sleet last night... we'll be looking for dad

and Bill Stanley early in the spring. P.S. Cecil says to bring some cigarettes-he may be short by March. Signed Cecil and Edna

Another later letter written by Edna about six weeks later was also recovered. On that day in 1933 she wrote to her in-laws *Well this is almost a summer's day so we'll send you a letter to tell you we are all well except Mary. She seems to have the mumps. There is very little ice in the pond...Cecil and Clifford built a new ice sled in case we get some cold weather. It doesn't look that way now. Hope you are all well. The men are in a hurry so good-bye. Love to All Cecil and Edna.*

Getting back and forth between the island and the main land then as now could be a challenge. In the spring of 1919, before the Coles had built their own vessel, King Cole hired a boat for the first trip of the season. He took along a couple of fish hatchery workers who planned to release a number of fish fry and they set out from Cape Vincent one calm mild late March morning. But March weather is fickle and after reaching the island to check on the care takers and releasing the fish they decided to head immediately back to the mainland as the wind was picking up.

About an hour from safety the engine quit. According to a story in the local newspaper the carburetor went wrong. The men "took the engine down and started to repair the wrong" but before they could finish the job it was too dark to work. Rolling and bouncing around in the increasingly cold wind they opted to anchor. It snowed and blew all night and no one got any sleep. Says the local paper three of the four "experienced the sensation of seasickness though all were trained sailors." They stuffed old rags into one of the fish hatchery cans and soaked them with kerosene and burned them for warmth and at some point their anchor line broke setting them adrift. After a miserable night daylight finally arrived and the engine was speedily "made right" so they could get home.

Though that particular passage had a happy ending others ended near the island under less fortunate circumstances. There are legends concerning a small French warship sailing to Fort Niagara with supplies and a pay chest of gold for the troops that was wrecked in late fall here around 1750. The story goes that the following spring searchers found on Main Duck a row of fresh graves, the last of which was empty. Presumably the man who had buried his fellows had dug his own grave, then perhaps wandered off to die alone. The gold if it ever existed was never found though history holds that a large boulder marked with a date and an arrow marked its burial spot. If that rock is still there it's too well concealed in the brush and shrubbery for me to find it.

Two twentieth century ships left their bones upon the shoal pointing west from the light house, the *Sarniadoc* and the *Hickox,* and some of those rusting remains are clearly visible yet today. Another visible reminder of the lake's wrath lies in School House Bay, the wooden ribs and planks of the steamer *Randall* that sank in 1920. She had anchored here for shelter on November 16 only to have the wind shift into the north and drive her ashore. One account says her stern hit a rock and her engine lifted up and she broke in two. The crew of four scrambled forward where the bow was still above water and remained there for ten hours washed by heavy seas and lashed by a November northeaster.

The ship's company finally made it ashore by means of a hatch cover and were found by one of the light house keepers. The four men stayed with the lighthouse tenders for nine days before they were picked up. Ironically a year and eight days after the loss of the *Randall* her Captain went down while in command of the *City of New York*. His wife and ten month old daughter went with him. Today rounded polished lumps of coal still wash up on the island's beaches.

In 1921, the year after the *Randall's* wreck, Claude Cole typed a letter to Ottawa in support of establishing a life saving station on Lake Ontario. It reads as follows;

In regards to the life saving station would say I had a long talk with the boys who are fishing there at the Island the season through and they are quite willing to give any assistance they can. Had there bin a life saving station there when the steamer John Hall went down a few years ago I could no doubt have saved the whole crew there was ten lives lost at that time.
    There has bin a lot of boats stranded on that Island since I have owned it, I would think about two a year.
    It is called the grave yard of Lake Ontario you can see three wrecks from where the beech makes at the head of the pond this I would say is a very natural place for a life saving station it is narrow at this poticular place one could go to either side of the Island he might choose having good protection on either side to start from
    I might also add that a Wireless Telephone should be erected in connection with life saving station as most all the Boats have a wireless

already on them and no doubt would be a very great aid to navigation the marine men are trying very had for this and if you remember last fall the critisism the marine department got for not having some way of communication from an isolated Island, like that of the crew that was given up for lost. They had not bin heard from for eight days that was the case of the Steamer John Randell wich was lost last fall. I would be willing to let the department have this piece of land for a station for the sum of one dollar per month the building they errect if ever abandoned to become my property. Sincerely yours C. W. Cole

The punctuation is Mr. Cole's perhaps his period key got sticky. The steamer *John Hall* he refers to went down about fifteen years before just to the southwest of the islands. The U.S. life saving station at Big Sandy on the lake's east end had been closed about three years before and efforts were made to move that station's equipment to the Galloo islands where a Coast Guard Station was located. But neither attempt to continue the rescue service were successful. By the 1933 Main Duck did have a radio navigation beacon and a radio telephone was installed at Galloo Island.

The current Main Duck light established in 1915 was for a time the most powerful on the lake. Willis Metcalfe published an account of the light in 1933 in a Canadian newspaper that closely resembled its condition in 1984 just before automation. By 1984 it was electrified thanks to a diesel generator housed next to the tower, but the rotating lenses and the open steep steel stairs and last little leg to the top by ladder were little changed and the 55 pound weights and clockwork mechanism that once turned it were still at least partly in place, though no longer needed.

Metcalfe noted that thousands of bags of cement and tons of steel were used in the tower's construction. "To ascend to the top of the lofty light one must climb three flights of steel stairs, erected in zig-zag fashion. And many persons when descending these steps have lost their nerve and have had to be carried down them with much difficulty."

Metcalfe described the prism lenses and the works of the light as weighing over seven and one half tons and being of the revolving type. "It floats on two and three-quarters gallons of (quick-silver) mercury. This metallic fluid is drained out each year and strained through five thicknesses of flannel cloth. In the interior of the light is a five-inch mantle which burns on part air and coal oil, consumption being one gallon every eight hours...The gleaming panels revolve slowly and radiate a broad white flash every six seconds to guide ships through perils of the night. Situated in the tower beside the light is a twenty-inch glass case which houses the governing mechanism, this regulating the revolving speed of the light.... "

In 1933 Main Duck had not yet been electrified as had neighboring Galloo, although the light house did have a "wireless telephone" by then, and the fog station was operated by compressed air and had two twelve horse power kerosene engines to compress the air stored in tanks. Of course the keeper had to keep the massive Fresnel lenses polished and we assume he had to lug that kerosene up all the stairs daily.

Perhaps by 1984 they had dispensed with filtering the mercury, but it was still there and the whole works intricately turning and flashing and shining in the September sun inside the glass chamber of the tower was like a beautiful sculpture when I saw it. I figured that day as I turned and looked out over the bright blue lake and white lines of surf refracting over the shoal just west of the light that I would be one of the last yachters to ever climb the tower with a keeper as guide and enjoy that view. The light was automated the following summer one of the last on the Great Lakes to have been manned.

In 1929 a few years after Cole tried to have a life saving station established he went in search of another lost mariner. He sought an old acquaintance Benjamin Kerr the "well known exporter of Hamilton Ontario" as the local newspaper termed him. Ben Kerr was one of the lake's most successful rum runners and he and his assistant on the *Pollywog* were seven days overdue from an early March departure from Presqui'le with "cargo" for Rochester. His wife wired Cole and asked if he would assist in the search and Cole immediately secured an airplane and flew the lake from Watertown west nearly to Presqu'ile.

It was a clear and calm day and the men saw deer, ample expanses of unbroken ice and circled several islands during the nearly two hour flight, but no sign of the men appeared and Cole told Mrs. Kerr as reported in the local paper "It does not seem possible they will ever be found alive...It would not surprise me much if the two men were unloading near the American shore that a machine gun might have been turned on them, or they might have hit a large cake of ice and gone down." About a month later the mystery of Kerr's disappearance ended as Cole received a letter from Kerr's brother that stated "Last Thursday they found the body of Alf Wheat and parts of the boat and on Saturday morning found my Brother's body near Cobourg…Once again I thank you for your kind co operation and sympathy."

In the waning days of Prohibition things got pretty nasty between rival gangs and rum running was not the casual cottage industry of its early days when my old Watertown neighbor Leo Garlock and his buddy Mike ran their pokey little open boat back and forth between Ivy Lea and Oswego as detailed in *Ariel's World*. The easy and lavish profits powered organized crime and plenty of killing and Kerr had run afoul of a number of "businessmen" in his dealings that wanted him gone. Perhaps he was hijacked or perhaps the lake got him. The letter to Cole didn't say.

Cole was prickly and independent minded, but generous, warm-hearted, and hospitable to island visitors and to the occasional yacht seeking safe haven. (One visiting yachter caught by bad weather reciprocated by presenting Cole with his boat's entire stock of reading material when he departed). "King" Cole was widely respected and liked. As one account of the island written shortly before he died stated "the Main Ducks with or without its wrecks will be interesting as long as it is dominated by so genial a king as Claude Cole."

After Claude Cole died in 1938, his son Cecil continued the islander lifestyle until his own death from a heart attack and then, according to Willis Metcalfe's account, "international lawyer" John Foster Dulles (who grew up in Henderson Harbor and visited Main Duck as a boy sailing over in his small boat,) purchased it. Of course, the cold war warrior later became Secretary of State and Main Duck became the retreat of the wealthy and powerful who went hunting and fishing together and presumably told stories and made deals over their drinks around the fireplace of Dulles's modest log cabin.

Today only the chimney and a bit of foundation remain and Main Duck re-purchased by the Canadians, is now a park island. But the view from the overlook where once Dulles relaxed is as splendid as ever. Main Duck with its rockbound shores and low sometimes barren wind swept interior is not a soft or gentle place. For a few months in the summer though, it shows a gentler side- a place where summer flowers flourish briefly and bobolinks and field sparrows call over the "grasslands" while crystal clear water ripples over the stone ledges.

We lingered in the hot June sun by the lighthouse peering into the channel where the big bronze carp slip stealthy in and out of the shallow warm lagoon they like so much. Watching them sneak past us and seeing the gulls overhead, I wondered aloud perhaps we'll come back as gulls and visit Main Duck in another life. We'll probably come back as carp said my partner who admires their underwater brawn and speed. No it'll be as birds. Perhaps as loons. They like less populated places. They go their own way. We'll come back as loons and cry in the summer twilight over the water by Main Duck.

On the way back to the boat walking on the beach I picked up two stones. One beach pebble had a round hole though it, the other contained a spiral fossil shell, created five hundred million years ago in the shape of our galaxy.

Never Say Oops In Front Of A Customer

In 1997 after acquiring part ownership in a 32 foot fiberglass sloop of classic design, I decided to go "commercial". I thought our handsome sweet sailing yacht would be a great vehicle for introducing other people to the wonders of Lake Ontario. I also had some vague notions that through sailing people would realize how splendid, fragile and precious these waters were and that this new appreciation might eventually translate into advocacy and political action on behalf of the lake. In a few instances some of these hopeful ideals actually were fulfilled. But not usually. Life seldom goes exactly as we visualize or plan. I guess that's what keeps it interesting.

To go commercial and to put the good ship *Titania* to work, I had to first obtain my Coast Guard license to carry passengers for hire. This is the document that allows you to legally collect payment for taking people for a ride aboard an auxiliary powered sailboat. Little did I know then what lay in store in the way of unseen reefs and tide rips off my bow. I thought getting my "ticket" would be dead easy.

Lake Ontario at the dawn of the twenty first century abounded in fishing charter boats, each commanded by a certified "captain". In 1996 a Sea Grant survey estimated that they annually contributed approximately 56 million dollars to the local economy. Most charged several hundred dollars per passenger for a half day of fishing. It sounded like an easy way to pick up a little supplemental income while doing something I enjoyed and did anyway.

At the time I decided to obtain my license there were about 300 fishing charter businesses on the lake's NY shore and probably about a dozen sailing operators. The balance of fishing to sailing charters should have suggested something to me about the relative demand for and profitability of the two services. I knew of only one female captain who took passengers for hire. (I've since then encountered several others.) Nearly all the Lake Ontario charter industry, fishing and sailing alike, operated as hobby businesses with most captains using their own boats. Some of those sailed with a mate or crew but many single-handed as I planned to do. They were retired business execs, union workers, fire fighters or other pensioners, or they worked at their seasonal fishing business as a supplement to other income (which, of course, I as a freelance writer also aspired to do).Very few were full time. According to Sea Grant in 1994 the Lake Ontario fishing charter boats averaged a gross income of 15,016 dollars and spent about 11,154 dollars. An actual pretax profit of $3962 sounded pretty good to somebody selling 1000 word articles at ten cents a word!

Back in 1994 charter boats surveyed by Sea Grant generally had to make at least 40 trips a year (about twice as many trips as I ended up usually doing) to make a profit and about half of the boats operated at a loss. Since the Sea Grant survey the Lake Ontario fishery has been in a mild decline, at least from an economic perspective, so I suspect the average profitability has dropped further. Most charters were for salmon though some Lake Ontario skippers also took their boats out with paying customers for bass. Generally they ran from April through September, a somewhat longer season than I would be able to do with *Titania*. I had no real aspirations of making a living at my supplemental profession but I did hope to get our fine new boat to at least pay her expenses.

Before I went commercial myself, I had watched the "fish heads" thunder past on Saturday afternoons, their powerful boats gaudy with tackle maker decals and fishing rod lures that twinkled in the sun. I had a low (and inaccurate) opinion of their general level of seamanship since most of them seldom operated over an hour's high-speed run from safe harbor. If they can carry passengers for hire and collect several hundred dollars for a half day's work, I thought, surely a highly educated and intelligent person such as myself can manage to obtain a license and quickly grow rich (or at least break even) while teaching about Lake Ontario. I subsequently radically reevaluated my opinion of their level of competency!

In 1996 a considerable cottage industry flourished in my area that was devoted to the business of preparing would be captains to take the Coast Guard exam to qualify for their "ticket". I called up an acquaintance who taught in one of these captain's schools located in Oswego, a hot bed of recreational salmon fishing. "Hey", he said, "it's not that easy. It'll cost you a thousand dollars to get that license." He proceeded to reel off a lengthy list of requirements for the applications process- finger prints, eye exam, notarized references, urine test for drugs, proof of citizenship, sea time documentation, physical, etc. adding that I couldn't possibly do this on my own without his classes. I hung up sobered. I didn't have a thousand dollars. That's why I wanted the license- to make some money!

Then I called another friend, one with a hundred ton license that allowed him to operate dinner boats and other so called Inspected Vessels as well as the smaller UPV (uninspected passenger vessel) that the typical fishing charter skipper employs. "YOU can do it- it's easy! Just some simple set and drift charting problems, learn the rules of the road cold and it's not that hard." In retrospect, I think friend number 2 had heard a few too many of my sea stories from my days of single handing *Ariel* around the lake and had formed an inflated picture of my seafaring know-how.

So I sent off for the application package, thinking if all I had to do was pass a test, I had a fair chance of success. I'd spent a large portion of my adult life in an academic environment delaying my entry into the World of Work for as long as possible. And I'd taken countless civil service exams after finally leaving school in my quest for a Real Job with bennies like a pension and health insurance. I wasn't confident of my ability to tackle many of life's challenges, but boy I knew I could take a test- SAT's, GRE's, Master's orals, Civil Service Fisheries biologist, NTE, I'd passed 'em all. What I probably really needed was a career in taking tests.

But after I'd waded through the application for taking the Coast Guard test, which made Federal Income Tax form 1040 with schedules A,B,C,D,E and forms 4562 and 4797 all of which I'd managed to fill out after a fashion over the last five years, a cakewalk by comparison, I revised my estimation of the upcoming exam's difficulty. It had been far easier to get clearance for work in the Ginna nuclear plant as a firewatch than to get on the list to take this lousy test! One thing is certain, to be a licensed Captain you must be able to read government English and follow directions!

At last, after a couple of tries, the application with 85 dollar fee had been mailed off and approved. It was now January of 1997 and I had set my sights on a license by spring so as to put *Titania* to work that year. Time to study! A friend noticed a study guide in one of his marine equipment catalogues. I ordered Gonder's Charters West home study guide, and settled in by the woodstove for many a winter's evening of set and drift, maneuvering signals, and running fixes. As the snow piled up on my boat's cover and the wood pile in the garage dwindled, I memorized whistle signals and mast head light visibilities. However, as the first redwing blackbirds returned with a late winter thaw, I was far from ready for the test.

The exam I was studying for was for the entry level "operator of uninspected vessels" license to 25 ton (identical to the widely used "six pack" license except for the open book part) and consists of several Modules. The charting section contained ten questions that you worked with a test chart and excerpts from Coast Pilots and Light lists to answer. Some of these charting questions were straightforward asking you to look up information in the Coast Pilot or Light List, others required plotting, converting compass courses, and figuring set and drift. Even the "easy" questions such as what is the height of tide at such a time and place may contain sneaky little twists like reading the fine print about daylight savings.

The second section of the exam consisted of 30 inland and International rules of the road questions. Miss 3 maximum and you still pass. I missed 3. This, most candidates agree is the hardest part of the exam. Then there are sections of navigation aids and chart symbols, optional towing, and sailing addenda and the 60 questions requiring general knowledge of such things as anchoring, traveling on rivers, tides, weather, ship and boat handling, safety and some specific knowledge that I didn't have a clue about.

For one thing, there were all these ship questions on my mock tests in the practice book. I didn't know the flash point of crude oil or what the required minimum bursting pressure on a 2.5 inch transfer hose should be. And how could I find out? With my spring deadline looming I began to panic. I called on another acquaintance who also taught courses for license candidates. How the heck would I know how many fire extinguishers are required in the machinery space of a small inspected passenger vessel powered by diesel or what hose burst pressure on a tanker should be? "You don't". he said. "You look it up in something called the CFR's (Code of Federal Regulations). That's the open book part of the test. You can find the code at any Government Documents library." He then explained the CFR format, told me the applicable volumes and loaned me a set of four "parts" that contained much of the material I would need to look up during the exam so I could thumb through them and get an idea of how they were organized.

At last, heartily sick of day shapes, set and drift, and Honolulu tows, I signed up for the Big Day. I got up at 2 am, ate breakfast, and on a raw day in March drove to the test location in Buffalo and followed the herd of condemned down into a slightly clammy basement of an old armory building. Five hours later it was over. I had passed the exam. Quite honestly, it was one of the hardest I'd ever taken. It ranked right up there with the orals for my Masters in Fisheries. Maybe I was getting old and intellectually brittle, but as I drove home that day I was much humbled. I, ace test taker, had been nearly undone by this entry-level kindergarten of the mariner's arts.

While much of seamanship and competence comes from a combination of experience and judgment, not from a piece of paper that says you have a license, I also now had far more respect for the specialized training and knowledge of those commercial vessel operators, dinner boat captains, and yes, even for those charter fishermen.

Once I was a legal "Captain" I opted to offer both sailing lessons and charters. I purchased a fiberglass Lightning, a vintage Lippincott-built hull number 11190, and acquired ten copies of the Red Cross learn to sail basic guide to re-sell to students as a text. The Lighting was a 19-foot racing dinghy with a large cockpit. She was quick and lively and ideal for basic instruction. I figured bigger heavier *Titania* would act as charter boat. In actuality both boats acted as instructors. The Lightning took most of the lessons, while *Titania* and I generally made perhaps a dozen or so day trips and sunset sails a season. *Titania* also did a few overnight "live aboard and learn" instructional cruises with couples and small groups. Most of the day trips were with couples. But we also sometimes carried families, singles, grandmothers, and small groups of friends. Through the years, several dogs also took passage.

The first to take a dogwatch was a large yellow lab who signed up in my second season of chartering. During the phone call to make a reservation, the owner asked hesitantly if there was any chance of bringing the dog along. We had just had a cousin's dog aboard and all of us had survived, so I told the dog owner I was game. Just be sure he wears a harness so we have something to grab him by if he tries to jump ship I advised.

It was an exceedingly hot day of gentle winds and nearly smooth seas, and after we managed to wedge the slightly bewildered but willing animal in the cockpit, we dumped buckets of water on him to cool him off. While we didn't have a lot of room for our feet, putting him down there did keep him from sliding around and as long as we kept him wet he was reasonably comfortable. I'm not sure the whole affair was his idea of a grand time, but he did his best to be a good sport. I think a walk on the beach with some nice dead fish around to chew on would have been a lot more fun.

The other dog who took a sailing trip was Lady, an 80-pound German shepherd. Her owner wanted to buy a sailboat. But, he figured, first he had to see if his dog enjoyed sailing. Only then would he spring for the new hobby. Apparently as an afterthought, he decided to bring his wife too, though apparently it was a given that she would go along with the idea of sailing.

Lady showed up in her brand new life jacket and after debating whether to leap over or crawl under the lifelines, she did manage to get aboard. At a still gangly one year of age, she was longer legged than the lab and didn't fit down in the cockpit very well, so we settled her on a seat. She was willing and well behaved and spent most of the two hour trip with her head on her owner's knee and her butt parked squarely on the wife's lap. Once or twice she stood up and peered down at the water alongside, trying to figure out if it was worth jumping off and trying to walk home.(Unlike the lab, Lady had never been swimming and had probably never even waded in a body of water larger than a farm pond). The first time or two when we tacked and the sails rustled and rattled and the boat tipped the other way she got a little worried, but after a couple of tacks, she settled right in. The cruise was considered a success, by the humans at least, and Lady subsequently was seen sailing the bay aboard the couple's 21 footer. I was still picking long black hairs out of the mainsheet and the cockpit drains a week later.

Sometimes charters turned into impromptu sailing lessons and while *Titania* wasn't quite as nimble as the little Lightning, she was quick and responsive enough to do a pretty fair job given an 8 to 10 mile an hour breeze. On one such occasion a small family from New Jersey came aboard for a sail. None had ever been aboard a sailboat before but their 12-year old son wanted to learn to sail. When they first phoned, I suggested they try enrolling him in the local yacht club junior sailing program, however scheduling did not allow for that option. So they called back and we decided to at least get him out for one boat ride.

At the dock father asked if there was room for the cooler. I said sure and he went to get it, on return dragging a chest the size of a small refrigerator down the dock. I eyed it warily and hoped it wasn't full of beer. It wasn't. I should have figured that with an 8 and 12 year old they wouldn't be heavy drinkers. Once underway we put Mark (all names of customers herein changed to protect innocent and guilty alike) on the helm and let him take over. To my surprise the youngster really did want to learn to sail. He asked excellent questions, figured out the winches and the cleating the jib sheet operation simply by observation and he winched tailed and hauled on halyards with a will. He even insisted on going back to the mooring with the boat and picking up the pennant with the boathook. He then rowed his father ashore in the dinghy.

While on the tiller he steered a straight true course, unlike many beginners, and soon he was tacking *Titania* like a pro. The day was gentle and warm with a soft five to ten mile an hour breeze. While Mark steered close hauled, his mother and little sister went up on the foredeck and father settled back for a sun tan on the lazarette. Mark won me over when he announced upon clearing the harbor and seeing the lake before him, "I like it up here! I'm going to move here, buy a boat, live on it and go sailing all around the lake."

After an hour or so, he took a break from being helmsman and went forward to hang out with his sister. His mom came aft to be sociable. As we slipped quietly along, she noticed a motorboat adrift nearby. I followed her gaze to see a couple of sunbathers stretched out on the aft bench seat. Neither appeared to have any clothes on and they also appeared to be of opposite sex and in very close association with one another in what used to be delicately termed a compromising position. "Oh" I said to mother- "they're just getting a tan." Staring at the snow white buttocks she said "I don't think so." About that time *Titania* made a polite little "ahem" noise with her bow wave, and the couple hastily de coupled and assumed innocent sunbathing postures. "My son would have to see that." sighed Mother. I assured her, "he is twelve and he probably knows more than we think!" Afterwards I wondered what the vacationers told their friends back in Jersey about the lusty boaters of Fair Haven.

I also wondered how it was that a kid who had never been on a sailboat before would decide that he wanted to catch the wind and sail with it. Did *Titania* touch a life and shift its course even as mine was forever changed by my first turn at the helm of a boat belonging to a family friend thirty some years before? If so, I surely hope sailing enriches Mark's life as much as it has mine.

Another person who had a life changing moment at *Titania's* helm was Laura, a young Mom who had moved recently from the Midwest and purchased an 18 foot boat on e Bay. She was anxious to start sailing her new possession and so signed up for a lesson. We sallied forth with my Lightning who proved on this day of puffy and shifty warm southwest winds, to be quite a lively handful for the new student. As the morning went on, Laura mastered tacking but still found jibing involved a few too many things happening a little too fast to keep track of easily. I was watching the sky darken in the southwest and recalling a forecast of possible showers, suggested we take a lunch break aboard *Titania*. As we ate our sandwiches, the sky cleared so we decided to go back out for a bit more practice on the bigger ballasted boat.

The wind had shifted a bit more into the west so after Laura took the helm and sailed the boat off the mooring and tacked her out into the bay, she was able to coax the sloop out close hauled through the narrow entrance channel with no further tacking. This was a good test of her concentration and she worked hard keeping the boat close to the wind and sailing in a straight line. Then as we cleared the ends of the jetties I started the sheets a bit and told her to lay off the wind a few degrees. The boat accelerated and took off romping joyously through the two to three foot chop. She smacked into one wave and sent a bit of spray back and Laura feeling the scend of the larger ballasted yacht and its reassuringly surefooted response to a puff of wind exclaimed "This is great! I love it- I haven't had this much fun since my last kid was born!"

We sailed on lunging over the waves and heeling to the warm west wind under a hazy sun and my student began making plans to get her new boat up onto the wider waters of Lake Ontario asap. She was hooked just as I had been the first time I took the helm. I remember feeling that same sort of instant affinity that she had felt. "I like this" I thought then. I still think that today. There's something almost magical about the way of a boat under sail and about one's ability to direct and control this wondrous creation as it masters wind and waves. I have probably left the channel and sailed out onto open water a thousand times or more, yet each time I do I still feel that same exhilaration and joy that *Titania's* student driver felt for the first time that afternoon.

Some of the people who decided to learn to sail told me they had wanted to try it for many years before actually signing up for a lesson. One who had deferred the desire perhaps the longest of any, also reminded me of one of life's little lessons about making snap judgments. Harold's wife called me one summer morning and declared that it was imperative that I take her husband sailing. They had been at the shore the weekend before and watched the white winged sloops and gaily striped catamarans out on the blue water and, she told me "He's drooling. He has to get out on a sailboat. I have to get him out". We set a date and when I met them a few days later the wife introduced me to my student and told me firmly "He's an old man. Don't lose him overboard!"

Harold was a gray haired grandfatherly sort. He was an inch or so shorter than me which makes him pretty short. He had a cheerful face and bright blue eyes and he smiled as we were introduced. It was a brutally hot muggy afternoon hazy with a shifty puffy southwest wind. As I gazed upon this "old man" as his wife called him I thought oh boy, I wonder how this will go. We boarded the Lighting and I saw that my pupil was agile and surefooted moving around the boat. His sharp eyes noticed details most beginners overlooked as we rigged the boat, though he was a quiet student not given to much talk or many questions. Once we began to sail, he steered straight and steady and tacked unerringly right from the start.

I was impressed and asked him have you been sailing before? No he answered, but I watch the sailboats all the time. When a puff came along and the little Lightning accelerated skimming along over the water his face lit with pleasure as he said, "This is nice." The first time or two he had a bit of trouble shifting sides until I showed him he could lift up the tiller and duck under it. He was otherwise as nimble as I in moving about the boat. After an hour of sailing in the variable winds under challenging conditions for a beginner I had completely revised my opinion of my student. He picked up the basics of sailing faster than almost anyone I'd ever taught in six years. He had owned several motorboats in years past on Long Island Sound and elsewhere and he had used a canoe for sometime. But sailing had fascinated him since he was a boy. He had always wanted to sail. Now finally after a half-century or more of waiting, he was at the tiller.

He was soft spoken with an old world politeness and formality and said little except when spoken to. Except when it came time to tack. Then he would murmur quietly "prepare to tack" and when I had uncleated my jib sheet and said "ready" he would push the tiller over firmly and rap out a firm authoritative command "Tacking!" It made me think of a clipper ship captain on his quarterdeck. After one lesson he had mastered techniques and maneuvers that many students needed two or three sessions to manage. And the sharp puffs and shifts didn't faze him a bit. He kept the Lightning footing along like a pro. I was reminded not to make snap judgments even as once again, the teacher learned from the student.

When I first began sailing for pay, charters didn't excite me as much as trying to teach people to sail. I was a little intimidated at the thought of playing the gracious hostess or salty old sea captain role for some possibly seasick passengers. To my surprise, I found boat rides turned out generally to be more interesting and enjoyable than I had expected. Frequently in answering questions I got an opening to talk about the lake and engage in a little teaching and lecturing, a role that I was comfortable with, and I soon learned that many of the landlubbers on vacation had an attitude that they were going to have a good time no matter what. And being in that mindset, they almost always did.

One memorable charter that occurred not long after I had pressed *Titania* into the passenger carrying business took place in August. It was a sunset sail after a particularly warm summer day and as I headed out into the lake with my two passengers, a middle aged husband and wife, we looked astern to the south at a mountain range of huge cumulous clouds towering high into the evening sky. As the soft south wind pushed us out of the bay and we turned west to reach along the shore, those distant heaped piles of vapor began picking up colors from the setting sun. After the sun grew ruby red and then slipped under the horizon the lofty clouds remained lit in delicate shades of soft gold and brass and rosy pink. We could also see heat lightning almost continuously flashing and pulsing within the massive bodies of vapor. To the east the golden disk of the moon rose over the ravaged eroded clay slopes of Sitts Bluff and began to lay down a bit of glitter on the nearly calm water.

We were entranced by the night's beauty as *Titania* slipped along with a light south wind over the calm lake. The incense like fragrance of wood smoke from state park campfires scented the air along with the rich fertile aroma from Sterling Creek Marsh. As the sky darkened and the moon lifted higher it laid a light path of shimmering silver upon the water. That soft light glowed luminous upon our white sails and clearly lit the shadowed deck. After a blistering burning hot day, we relished the gentle night and lingered on the lake well past the usual two hour sailing time.

Bewitched by the powerful moonlight, the gentle song of the bow wave and the soft steady wind, I enlisted my passengers to help tack *Titania* homeward through the channel. It was too perfect and too quiet a night to disrupt it with the putter of the motor so we sailed. One tack was favored but we still had to go around a couple times. In the still night we could easily pick up the rustle of *Titania's* bow wave reflecting off the jetty as she closed with its steel wall. Then we would see the side of the jetty in the glow of her running light about a boat length or so away. Ready about-hard alee and the yacht would spin around swiftly like a dinghy making her turn in a few yards with a rattle of sail cloth and the racket of a turning winch echoing off the steel wall. No other sound entered my awareness. It was a moment of total absorption and teamwork as we sailed down the passageway.

Thirty miles to the south the distant clouds still flickered and flashed with pulsing dull orange heat lightning while the moonlight silvered their rounded tops. We motored the last few yards through the night's coolness to the dock. Here we shook hands and bid farewell and parted presumably never to meet or speak again. But I still remember that night of perfect sailing when we all fell under the spell of the strong silver light of an August moon.

In the following summers of lessons and charters we sailed with nuns, a blimp pilot, several graduate students, a couple of Ph d biologists, an African missionary home on leave, a Ukrainian software engineer, a Columbian MBA student, and a Turkish electrical engineer. One quiet morning we sailed with Grandfather, Mom and little girl. When I inquired of the little girl "Are you ready to get on the boat now?" her mother told me firmly "Wrong question. At this age we don't ask them. We tell them 'Amanda, we're getting on the boat now!'" The toddler was actually very well behaved. She ate cherries and crackers, helped grampa steer the boat, and we sang several old traditional ballads of the sea like row row row your boat and baby white beluga where's your mom?

Some days we tacked and jibed until we were dizzy, a few days we sat and waited for the wind, and most of the time things went smoothly. But not always. I suppose everyone in this business has a few disasters and days like the one when I wrapped the mooring pennant on our prop and had to go overboard to clear it prompting one of the charter party to chide me with a grin "You should never say oops in front of a customer." One student fell off the dock while boarding the Lighting. It was a warm sunny day and she insisted on going through with the lesson wet clothes and all. Another time we lost a halyard up the mast after a student didn't attach the shackle properly. We got rained on once or twice and becalmed a few times and a few objects got dropped overboard, but luckily none of them were car keys or other irreplaceable treasures. And surprisingly few people got seasick.

A couple of the most gratifying charters we ever had involved "old salts" who had once sailed their own boats before the infirmities of age beached them. One such former boat owner upon trying a new therapeutic regimen for his severe arthritis found it so successful that he decided to see if he could still handle a boat. He chartered *Titania* twice, each time steering and trimming the main most of the trip. After the second sail he was so encouraged that he started making plans to look around for a small ballasted day sailor to get back afloat with.

The other old salt had been grounded by a stroke that impaired his mobility and his strength. He was left essentially one handed by it and able to walk with difficulty. His spouse was determined to get him back afloat and set up the charter partly to evaluate her own abilities to single hand the sailboat if need be. We corresponded by e-mail to determine the feasibility of getting him aboard and the accessibility of the dock and agreed to give it a try. That day *Titania* and I sailed with a couple whose quiet courage and devotion to each other left me humbled. To see a person so sorely beset yet work to recover and fan the spark back to life when dreams and hopes flicker low is something to remember.

Our first trip was on a gentle warm September day of blue skies and very little wind. Though the former skipper said little, mostly sitting quietly wedged by cushions in the cockpit, he apparently enjoyed the outing despite the lack of wind. His wife proved to be a very adept and capable sailor who had no difficulty managing *Titania* who was much larger than the boat they usually sailed on.

A year later they arranged for another sail. I wondered how I would find the old salt this time. Would he have kept his hopes afloat? Or like another old salt I knew, would his body have continued to decline and weaken leaving him beached permanently? This day of overcast sky and ten to fifteen knot winds was much more of a sailor's day than our outing had been a year before. And I could see as they approached, that the skipper was now shuffling unaided at a steady pace with his cane. He had not given up the ship. Far from it. Many hours of therapy workouts, swimming and exercise had paid off. That day as we sailed along the shore on a close reach over two to three foot steel gray waves under a low sky of stratus he took the helm for nearly the whole charter. *Titania* put her rail down and sailed at seven knots, surging over the waves, rising to them with a quick lift, but still sailing with light and mannerly helm. She seemed to be on her very best behavior that day and when his wife asked how he was doing the quiet man at the tiller responded with a smile like a shaft of sunlight breaking through cloud. He was very happy.

We sailed for over three hours that day and the old salt told me afterwards "I've got the fever again". He had felt the wind, raised his sails and steered a true course, and it had been good. I dropped them off at the dock and as we chugged back to the mooring I told *Titania* that we had just sailed with two greathearted folks. There go a couple of troopers down life's rough road. I hope I can remember their courage as they seek to live as fully as possible together.

When I had first pressed *Titania* and the Lightning into service as charter boats, I saw myself as a teacher and advocate for Lake Ontario. But somewhat to my surprise, along the way I found the boats and I were making people happy. And far from being a frivolous thing, it began to seem like an oddly worthwhile activity. When someone told me that their excursions on the Lightning and *Titania* had made their life richer, all I could think was that the feeling was mutual.

Yachts and their use are all about relationships, after all. At least for those yachts whose skippers don't sail solo. Relationships between customers and vendors, between husbands and wives, between parents and children and among friends occur on a boat. A quiet cockpit on a peaceful summer day fosters the all but forgotten art of leisurely conversation. And on sailing yachts at least, when people join forces and work together, the boat operates smoothly and nearly effortlessly. The sailing yacht also offers two of the essentials of the Bohemian way of life, beauty and freedom, and time to enjoy them as you travel along at 6 miles an hour. I found myself sharing things I valued greatly with my customers. And just as the cliché says, a thing shared becomes oddly greater and more satisfying.

I heard some remarkable stories and sailed with some exceptional people during my quest to make money with a boat. Those people gave me insights and appreciations that I would never have acquired on my own, and I'm lucky to have had the experience.

Old Salts And Bay Sailors.

Crustal rebound following the last ice age blessed Lake Ontario's south coast between Rochester and Oswego with a half dozen bays that are now centers of regional cottage life and recreational boating. The largest of these is Sodus Bay about five miles long. Little Sodus, (also known as Fair Haven and in the past called Ontario Bay) Irondequoit, and Port Bay are considerably smaller. Great and Little Sodus have had stabilized dredged entrances for over a century. East, Port, and Blind Sodus Bay rely on informal arrangements by property owner groups to keep small boat channels open.

These shallow protected areas are of vital importance to the overall ecology of the lake. Probably 90 % of the lake's total fish production takes place in less than 10 % of its waters in near shore shallows. Sunlight reaches to the bottom here and nourishes the growth of one celled algae and larger rooted aquatic plants. These in turn form the base of a food chain that reaches well out into the open lake. A number of fish species from the open lake also spawn in these protected waters and the young use them as a nursery ground. Various birds and animals make use of these bays, too, or at least did historically. Today, though, the main life form using most bay shoreline is *Homo sapiens* a species like many others attracted to warm shallow waters.

In the early part of the twentieth century there was substantial commercial activity and a sizeable subsistence economy based on the bays. Both Great and Little Sodus had active ports with coal trestles wharfs and grain elevators. There were also dozens of smaller businesses and jobs associated with the bays- commercial fishermen, ice cutters, boat builders and by 1900 a thriving tourism industry that kept things lively here. Boat liveries waterfront hotels and inns, dance halls and guest houses sprang up to accommodate visitors by the turn of the century.

Organized yachting on Lake Ontario goes back to the 1840s. In a competition for both sail and rowing boats off Toronto widely viewed in 1842, the yacht *Lapwing* beat the *Belle Louise* to take the prize for sailing boats. After the regatta, there was dancing and dinner with waltzes and quadrilles aboard the steamer *City of Toronto*. Yachting became a regular part of the scene around Lake Ontario with the founding of the Royal Canadian Yacht Club of Toronto about 1850, only five years after the first yacht club in America, the New York Yacht Club, was established. Soon other clubs were started on the U.S. shore at Charlotte, Oswego, and Sodus Bay. By 1884 there was enough organized yachting to establish an international racing organization, the Lake Yacht Racing Association which brought all the various clubs together for a series of races and parties each summer.

In the days of iron men and wooden ships freshwater yachting was quite a different activity than it is today. Not all Lake Ontario yachts were huge affairs manned by professional crews and paid captains and owned by millionaires. Some were modest sized and were sailed by strictly "Corinthian" crews comprised of businessmen, bankers, office workers, and other unpaid amateurs much like today's yachter. Increasingly by the 1880's industrialized America supported a middle class, and many of them were becoming Sunday Sailors. Sometimes several men would go in together to own a thirty to forty foot boat and then as now racing was a popular pastime.

Most early Lake Ontario races were long distance open lake competitions in boats that many modern day sailors would scorn as unsafe at worst and uncomfortable at best. Some yachts were little more than open keel boats subject to being swamped and possibly sunk by heavy seas. Others had closed off water-tight cockpits, but their cabins were frequently so rudimentary that the cruising yachters often took a tent along and camped on shore. Races, though, were every bit as competitive as they are today and cash prizes of a 150$ or more were awarded to the winner (at a time when 350 $ was a year's salary for a female school teacher). It's probably safe to assume there was also plenty of heavy wagering on race outcomes involving considerably greater amounts than the prize money. On salt water, wagers of a thousand dollars or more were commonly made on yacht races.

Irondequoit Bay's yachting suffered a blow when the railroad built a low bridge across its outlet, and before World War II Port Bay's shifting channel deterred use by anything more than small commercial and recreational boats. But Great and Little Sodus Bays had commercial port facilities and maintained channels dating to the mid 1800's. The Sodus Bay Yacht Club started up in 1893, and built its present clubhouse for 2200 dollars in 1900. At its formal opening the club history records that

Dr. Chamberlain's steam yacht and Mr. Vary's naptha launch gave rides around the bay to one and all. At midnight when the party ended, Commodore Meade provided transport to Newark for residents in his private railroad car. The club history goes on to quote a Newark Courier Gazette story "on the whole the club house is very satisfactory, although a few defects are noticeable". One of them was the lack of any toilet facilities. Perhaps this deficit had been rectified by the time the Sodus Bay Yacht Club decided to admit women to its membership rolls in 1905.The ladies were allowed to join as associates with dues of two dollars a year.

The current Fair Haven Yacht Club was established after World War II, though an earlier yachting association was in place by the early 1930s. The Fair Haven Yacht Club's first home was in the venerable Pleasant Beach Hotel. By the time the current club was established on its west side location in 1953 much of the sailing on Little Sodus Bay was done in small wooden "one design" sailboats like the Thistle, Lightning, Rhodes Bantam, and the Star. Many of these smaller boats were home built, sometimes from factory manufactured kits. Others were built by local shops like Triangle Marine on the Genesee River or Bill Kallusch boats of Sodus Bay or other area shops. The Barnes Brothers of Skaneateles, builders of several popular small racing boats, launched the first Lightning class sloop back in 1938. Sixty years later thousands of Lightnings were still being sailed around the world.

Back before plastic and the multitude of electric and electronic devices that make yachting easier and safer today, middle class yachters had distinctly different ideas of luxury. A 73 foot schooner yacht at the Rochester Yacht Club was noteworthy according to the club history for having sleeping accommodations for ten a "roomy galley" and an ice box with six hundred pound capacity. Auxiliary engines in the 1920's and 30's and fiberglass hulls and Dacron sails in the late 1950s and early 1960's made yachting less subject to the whims of wind and rot and broadened its appeal. After World War II many clubs started up active junior sailing programs to teach boys and girls to swim and sail their own little prams, Bantams, or Blue Jays. This also helped fuel a regional surge of interest in sailing on Lake Ontario in the 1960's. Thanks to fiberglass hulls, boats became far easier to care for and with increasing post war affluence and the rise of easy credit, most of the little wooden one designs soon gave way to larger fiberglass yachts with overnight accommodations and ballast like the lively J-24 or our own 1968 Chris Craft sloop *Titania*.

One long time Fair Haven resident and sailor June McArthur when asked what kids did back in the late 1950s and early 1960's on Fair Haven Bay remembered "Everybody went down to Buster's Boat Basin ". Here on the east side of the bay they fished, swam, water skied and did whatever teens and pre-teens gather in groups to do on long lazy summer afternoons.

There were two distinct groups of kids in Fair Haven back then according to June. There were the townies whose families were resident year around and the offspring of the summer people. And the two rarely mixed much, each tribe considering the other inferior. In the summer the teen aged townies worked at places like The Dairy Bar, the local grocery store, or they waited tables at the " P B " (Pleasant Beach hotel), the one still surviving waterfront restaurant. Some kids worked on farms picking strawberries and heaving hay bales. And some worked at the state park concessions, life guarded at the beach or drove the truck around the park that delivered ice cream and firewood to the campsites each day.

One thing Fair Haven kids did was spend a lot of time on the water both under power and sail. The bay had a tradition of pleasure sailing going back at least to the start of the twentieth century. Old photos show long ended gaffers and early one designs like the Star along with larger visiting yachts from nearby clubs and small Mackinac type boats under sail on the bay. June learned to sail with her stepfather George Green. "Half the kids on the bay learned to sail with him". He was apparently a good and patient teacher, for she recalls "He never yelled. Instead he'd say quietly in a conversational tone to the student who had just blundered badly "Now that didn't work. Let's try something else".

George told his stepdaughter that "You'll never be a good sailor until you capsize once." Years later she finally did turn a tiny Sea Snark over while sailing it in a stiff breeze, but George's boat always stayed right side up with her. George taught the youngsters aboard his 18 foot Robin, a sloop rigged one design popular in the area in the late 1920s and 1930s. The Robin class had a round bottom, a straight sheer, and a big cockpit. Several area boat shops including Kallusch's in Sodus Point and a shop in Skaneateles turned them out. Like the more widely built hard chine nineteen foot Lightning, also popular on Little Sodus Bay, the Robin was a good teacher.

June recalled that in her crowd, at least, the boys gravitated more towards power boating and liked to take George's eighteen foot runabout, a lapstrake Lyman Islander out for a spin. June was more likely to take the Robin out, particularly after one episode of wrapping the prop of the Lyman with the ski tow line. Asked about her sailing mentor and stepfather, she explained that he had grown up on and by the bay playing with pond boats as a child and tagging along with his father Wilbur Green the port's customs agent when he went down to check in a ship or yacht from Canada. The big two-story brick house on the hill over looking the bay where he grew up has a cupola said to have been designed as a vantage point to help customs keep an eye on the bay's comings and goings.

As a young man George worked as a lock tender on the canal and he was always interested in canals, even after assuming a career as an electrician. When the family took a Sunday drive or a vacation, they often ended up on some stretch of the barge canal or perhaps at a lock on the Rideau in Canada watching a boat pass through. To June the toddler, it was boring. But for bay sailor George there seemed to be an endless fascination with the idea of voyaging to distant lands. On a quiet summer evening June remembered "He'd often suggest to me 'lets go for a ride'. " They would then go down to the sturdy little Lyman step aboard and roar off through the bay and out into the lake. With the wide open waters and horizon before him he'd then ask her "Shall we go across?" As far as she knows he never did.

June recently wrote to me in a letter of her early memories of the bay as follows; "My parents, Brian and Winifred Stannard, were from Boonville and Constableville in the Adirondack Mountains. They moved to the Sterling area when I was four. My father had a job as a hired farm hand working for Gordon Longley in Sterling. Our farmhouse was a number of miles from the lake, but I remember going to both the Fair Haven State Park and the West Side. I remember one Sunday when our family went to the park for a day of swimming and a picnic with neighboring farmers, Mack and Alice Smith and their kids. Carol, my sister who was still in diapers, was sitting in three inches of water happily playing with a little bucket and spoon when a rogue wave came and pushed her over. Mack who was in his Sunday-going-to-church clothes - black shinny shoes with good pants and white shirt, jumped up off the blanket, and ran into the frothing waves to pick the wet screaming little girl out of the water. Carol, crying, clung to him until he handed her to our mother. Mack's clothes and shoes were soaked and covered with wet sand and seaweed and he had no change of clothes. In the warm summer weather they soon dried though.

People don't go to the park dressed up like that anymore, for good reasons too. When I look at Edna William's photos and see how they dressed to go to the beach I'm glad I didn't live back then. I can't imagine wearing all those clothes! Even when they went boating they appeared in their finest. I could never have kept myself that clean.

My whole youth was spent around Lake Ontario and the bay. We often went to the West Side of Fair Haven Bay, which was a spit of rocks and sand that grew from the dredging of the channel and the wave action around the piers. Alder, birch and weeping willow trees offered shelter from the sun and wind as we enjoyed the waters and the view. This rural beach was very special for all the families in the area who couldn't afford to pay the State Park admission fee.

In the summer, I would make sandwiches, sliced veggies, watermelon and Kool-aid for supper after we'd played in the water. My mother would soak and cool off from her hard day at the canning factory processing whatever was in season. Cherries, green beans, and peaches, she did them all. Many other families were scattered along the rocky beach, pier, and under the scrub trees. Some made fires to cook hot dogs or hamburgers.

The working class left their hot trailers and houses and went down to chill out by the lake. Children and dogs played together in the surf until the sky turned pink, gold, and chartreuse. People on the pier would wave at the lucky boaters who were heading out through the channel, with some kids chasing along the pier pretending they were in the bouncing boat. About the time darkness came so did the buzzing, bloodthirsty mosquitoes. Then it was a race for the car before we really wanted to pack up and leave.

There was always a way kids could get on the water if they didn't live in a waterfront house. The Red Creek Central School and the Red Cross offered a swimming program right after school was out in June. We froze learning to swim those early morning hours before the park opened to the day customers, a bunch of little kids with blue lips, wrapped in towels and shivering uncontrollably. They taught hundreds of us to swim, but I wish it could have been less painful.

My friend's grandfather, Ralph Stevenson was a keen fisherman, but he only took my friend Harriet and me along once. He was a quiet man, but I remember him swearing and smoking two packs of cigarettes during that excursion. We caught our hooks on every tree branch, root, bottom, and part of the boat. One of us even caught Grandpa Stevenson's jacket. He spent all his time unhooking our hooks and reloading worms for us. We had a great time, but had a lot to learn about not yanking on the pole the minute the bobbers bobbed. We'd get so excited at getting a bite that we'd yank and send the bobber, sinker and hooks zinging into the trees that draped over the calm water.

I belonged to the Campfire Girls and was very water oriented. Pat Westover, along with the help of her husband, Dick, and Assistant, Marian Ingersoll Green, taught us to fish and canoe. Dick was the ground's keeper of bay property owned by the Oswego State University. Marian Green owned adjacent land with a stream and horses (both features of the landscape always attractive to kids). We learned to hook our own worms, gather our own minnows and crabs, and remove our own fish from the hooks. We also learned how to paddle a canoe, forward and backwards, and also how to upright a capsized canoe, empty it of most of the water and paddle home. That came in handy years later when I began white water canoeing with my husband.

George Green, my stepfather, was the biggest influence water wise. When he came into my mother's life when I was in sixth grade, the whole bay and lake opened up to us. I was ecstatic! Here was a nice man who owned a Robin Sailboat and a Lyman inboard runabout. We could go to Buster's Boat Basin to swim and fish as well as have these boats that he'd take us out on every day after work. When George took time off in the summer we'd take day excursions with picnics and swimming.

As I got older and more proficient at boating he let me take the sailboat on my own. For some reason, even though he and I took the Coast Guard small boat course together, he didn't very often let me take the motorboat. The motor was a little tricky at times. He had the attitude that a woman could do anything, but I never did get down in the bilge and monkey around with the motor with him, like my brother did. I was able take the boat out if had a guy with me. But for wanting to take the boat out with just girls? Nada. Never.

Dating and marriage included a great deal of sailing and some motor boating. As a young teen, my husband Phil spent a week at the Fair Haven Yacht Club learning to sail on a village scholarship. The club sponsored a number of the local children. Phil also had an old wooden Chris Craft runabout while in college. Back in the early '60s he got away with storing it up in the marsh near Vaught Creek. The boat had a chronic leak from when Stretch Bonner had it. Phil would drive it up into the mud and it would only take on so much water before it hit bottom. He'd wade through the cattails to the bow of his boat and jump aboard, start it and take a little spin around the south end of the bay to get rid of the water and then come pick me up at the Little Sodus Inn or Pleasant Beach dock. Today a boat would probably be gone if it was left overnight like that.

Every place we've ever chosen to live in was because of its closeness to open water. As we traveled around the country in a camper, we settled in places that had water: The Florida Keys, Maryland, Austin and Corpus Christi, Texas, Fair Haven, and now Oswego, NY. We loved Taos, NM and Huntsville, Alabama, but they were too far from the water. Even in Austin, where there was Lake Travis, Lake Austin and Barton Springs we soon tired of them because we couldn't look across a great distance. Like my step-dad, I just wanted to know I could get out there and go and go, not that I ever have very often, but it's there."

After a long lifetime of boating, June's step father and bay sailor George passed on to Fiddler's Green at the dawn of the 21st century. His ashes were scattered over the waters he had spent so many happy hours on afloat sailing alone and with his family and friends.

The lake draws many to its shores. Another mariner who was a familiar sight on and by *Titania's* home port for over forty years was Buster Lozier, a handyman, carpenter, cottage builder, boat builder and businessman. Being a jack of all trades has always been a requirement for the successful entrepreneur, and Buster followed a long tradition in that regard. Though formally trained as a machinist, he sailed in the wake of other self-employed folk before him, a track marked by chance encounters, quick acquisition of new skills, and the development of strong relationships within a community. Many people knew Buster through his years of being the Boat Basin founder and operator, and his cheerful smile and ready stories made it a lively place on summer days.

Buster felt the draw of open water early on as he grew up a few blocks from the Niagara River. As a child the dramatic day to day changes of the powerful river fascinated him and he still recalls the spectacular collapse of the Honeymoon Bridge after a massive ice jam sixty feet thick swept away the concrete abutments. He arrived on the shores of Little Sodus Bay in 1949 after a brief and unsatisfactory stint handling hides in a shoe factory. Assembly line work did not suit this young worker, so aboard his 1930 Model A coupe with seventeen foot Old Town canoe lashed atop the pilot house he steered for wider waters.

Buster put in a couple summers building and renovating summer cottages and housing stock around Fair Haven. After World War II the village's decayed industrial past was fast giving away to residential development so business was brisk. Buster worked for a Mr. Grant who had purchased the entire parcel of railroad lands running from the village of Fair Haven almost to the State Park. Grant was selling off the waterfront in lots and Buster got one for himself tucked in behind Pearson Point. After buying his land, he had a thousand dollars left to build his house with.

He managed. Using rough lumber from a local mill and recycled rafters from a hotel being demolished he put up a simple little house beside what was to become a local institution and gathering place of waterfront watchers for fifty years-Buster's Boat Basin. Buster scrounged salvaged and made do to create his little marina. He built his docks himself and put together a fleet of six wooden flat iron skiffs. "I made a boat in a day and a half" he recalled. The skiffs rented for ten dollars a week, and soon paid back their cost. By 1955 the Boat Basin was a going business.

At the time at least two other businesses also offered anglers rowboats for rent. Bill Card at the Bay View Hotel had a fleet of carvel planked round bottom boats and the state park had a concessionaire who rented row boats. The bay was also home to several boat ride businesses during the 1940s and 1950s, predecessors to my Silver Waters Sailing. The longest running of these was that of Carl Foster. He ran a big mahogany launch equipped with a six cylinder Scripps engine. The boat would do about forty and was, so the story goes, similar to the model of a 1929 bootlegger. Foster charged 25 cents for a ride out in the lake, fifteen cents for a ride around the bay. Carl wanted to retire and offered the outfit to Buster for 1700 dollars but the busy owner of a thousand dollar house and the Boat Basin declined. He perhaps preferred to get out on the water with his own boat for fun. His first Lake Ontario boat was the *Blue Dew* a Popular Mechanix do-it-yourself design stretched from 17 to 21 feet.

In the 1950s Buster was one of tens of thousands of do-it-yourselfers building boats. Designs for back yard boat builders had been around since the 1890s and the Rudder Magazine published plans for a small sailing flattie the Lark around 1900. Even during the Great Depression people in pursuit of a dream kept building. World War II was only a temporary set back and amateur boat building got a boost in the 1950s from the availability of good grade affordable marine plywood. The *Blue Dew* like many boats of her day, was built of plywood covered with that new fangled fiberglass cloth and resin stuff.

With a five horsepower engine the *Blue Dew* wasn't fast, but she was seaworthy and survived more than one rough passage in and out of the bay. Buster recalled a summer day bass fishing with his buddy Wilbur up by second bluff. The lake was flat without a ripple but Buster, feeling something was coming looked off to the west to see an ominous fast advancing cloudbank. He and Wilbur scrambled to up anchor and get underway but the low powered little *Blue Dew* sailing against sixty mile an hour gusts was no speed boat. By the time she reached the breakwaters the seas were steep breaking five footers.

"I had a hatch cover up there that wasn't fastened down. I sent Wilbur up (below decks) and told him hold it down Wilbur. He wasn't too swift. He lost it." As the little *Blue Dew* climbed over the steep breakers taking spray but still no solid water over the bow, the crew hastily unearthed and rigged an umbrella over the opening to deflect most of the spray.

Blue Dew soon made way for bigger better boats including a 27 foot Garwood speedboat and a sweet lined little 26 foot Richardson cabin cruiser called the *Friend Ship*. She made a rough crossing with Buster and crew from Galloo Island to Oswego one very long dark night after the wind shifted and drove them from the island's north side anchorage. Once with his last boat, a 27 foot Owens, Buster got caught by a wave

off the end of the breakwater that rolled him over so far that the edge of the deck was in the water. She recovered, but it was a tense moment.
Others who ventured out that channel were less fortunate, and Buster recovered several victims' bodies during his years by the bay. "I got a lot of respect for the lake" he said recalling several tragedies he'd witnessed.

Buster also had a keen interest in the area's history. He found and saved various Indian artifacts including stone net sinkers and a stone hatchet while excavating the boat basin, and he listened to the stories of the older "water rats" who had watched over the port and bay back when it was host to commercial shipping. He recalled some of those tales including ice cutting with a Model T engine powered buzz saw, a fire at the coal trestle that burned two ships, the sinking of the freighter *Conger Coal,* and bootleggers who dropped their weighted bags of booze into the shallows of Meadow Cove for confederates to recover. He also chuckled over stories and memories of small town characters like Bill Jeffers who kept a small pet alligator at his little marina on the west side of the Bay, of Elmer the last light house keeper who was certain that he had ghosts in his bayside home, and of Bob Hill an old bachelor who loved opera and made the best fudge in the county. "They sewed him into his long johns in the fall and he took them off come spring".

In 1996 Buster sold his boat basin and retired to drop anchor just outside the village. At the time of my visit he was still planning to get his Owens back in the water though. And he was still telling stories that made people smile.

These days the bays and near shore waters lack the varied bustle of 75 years ago. Lake watchers no longer hear the distinctive thump of the trot liners' little hit and miss one-lungers as they head out to check the catch, nor does the racket of the coal car shaker echo off bay shorelines. But pleasure boats still draw foaming wakes and spread their white wings upon blue waters just as they did then.

 Most of us who sail the lake try to avoid it in its really nasty moods. Our passages and stories about them are usually (hopefully) less dramatic than those of the "old days". But there's still risk out there. Every summer boaters die on the big lake. There's still plenty of reason to overhaul your gear each spring, examine those fittings with a critical eye and perhaps replace an ageing sail before it can blow out at a time when you might really need it.

Through the years mariners have often regarded the vessels they sailed on as being more than mere objects. Boats have been seen as having an identity and spirit of their own for probably as long as people have built them. Even today some yachters personify their boats. The yacht takes us out onto a potentially hostile world, and we are grateful for her protection and strength as she overcomes big waves and strong winds. Yachts are also about power, control, beauty, and danger. And the yacht as she clears the channel and sets forth on wider waters is a means to adventure and freedom. It's heady stuff. Is it any wonder people still set sail upon inland waters? And once the day of sailing is over and the yacht safely anchored there comes that pleasant time of relaxing on deck supervising the close of day. As one yachter wrote a century ago "How delightful after a hard day's scrap, to make a quiet harbor and then visit one another's boats and in a comfortable cabin to sit and spin yarns…"

So as you conclude your passage upon this literary bark with Captain Sue and other shipmates and head ashore, I say thanks for coming along. May you enjoy fair winds on your future lake passages and a good yarn afterwards.

Photo section on Fair Haven Bay all photos by Edna Williams
Introduction by June MacArthur

Edna Williams, the photographer, was a woman born during the wrong century. She was born in 1873 and discovered the camera in its earlier days when she saw the need to photograph her environment. She had an eye for composing her subjects and sought them out actively. But she was born when women were supposed to be sheltered and not their own person. Women didn't have the vote and couldn't go out on their own, at least in Upstate New York villages of Sterling and Fair Haven if they were proper young ladies.

But Edna was one of several young women in the area that defied the norm. After a year of college and then teaching another year she left one of the very few jobs in the area then considered proper women's work and took to the shores and country-side with her box cameras. By the bay she photographed the sailing vessels, railroad locomotives and equipment workers, and other waterfront industry that would be gone in 50 years. Many of her photos were taken between 1900 and 1920 and used glass negatives and a heavy bulky outfit of camera negatives and tripod. Through her photos we can see the transition from horse and buggy days to the Ford model A's. The clothing of the children shows us how styles progressed through the 1900s through the 40s.

From her photos we can see the infancy of airplanes as her love for her son's marvel of flying took them through the countryside to all the fly ins and barn stormings they could find. And she preserved glimpses of rural life and the small self sufficient family farms that have vanished from upstate as completely as the passenger pigeon.

Williams made a little money with her photography; selling her postcards of some of the Lake Ontario shots and occasionally winning photo contests with the Syracuse papers. She also sold eggs from her large chicken stock. But she was mainly the housekeeper for the multi-generation home she lived at with her unmarried Aunt Eva, and Uncle Wilford Green, who adopted her illegitimate son, George Green, and their mother, Sarah Kosbeth Green, her grandmother.

These are just a few of Edna William's water front photographs. She took hundreds of photos of the area over the years but had a special love for Fair Haven and its waterways whether it was a stream with rowboats amongst lotus and cattails, the bay with ships steam or sail powered, and the Great Lake Ontario. I talked with Eddie Dennison, one of the youngest girls in many of the children photos and she said, "We loved it when we were spending the day with Aunt Edna and George. She'd pick us up in the morning with her jalopy, mother would have packed a picnic basket for us and we'd be off for the whole day, often not returning until after dark."

We hope you enjoy this sampling Edna William's pictures of Fair Haven Bay and Lake Ontario as we show a little of Edna's passage through her life in the early 1900s.

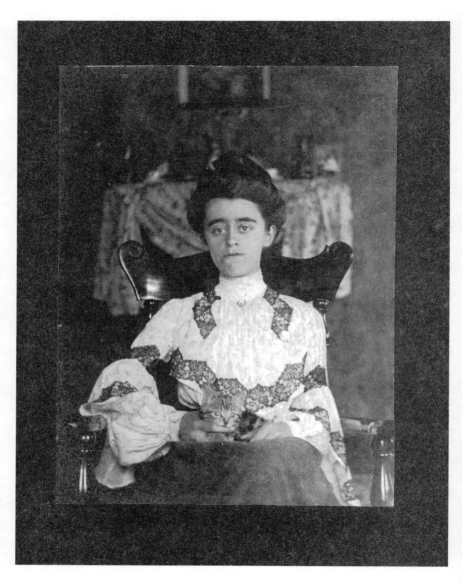

Edna Williams Photographer c.1905

Photographs

Light house tender *Crocus* along side the west pier after 1907 while behind her a dredge works to deepen the channel.

Before electrification of the two lights at Fair Haven *Crocus* made semi annual visits delivering supplies and fuel usually in the spring and the fall of the year. She also serviced buoys and later references to her on the internet refer to her as a buoy tender. Other Coast Guard tenders with botanical names from the time included *Hibiscus, Sundew* and *Maple*. Presumably the derrick on her foredeck was rigged for hoisting buoys on deck. Note the raised steel cat walk along the pier, another indication of the manned light era.

By this time the main port commerce consisted of shipments of anthracite coal. Coal from Sullivan and Luzerne counties in Pennsylvania arrived for shipment to various Canadian ports on Lake Ontario and the St. Lawrence. The harbor channel controlling depth was fourteen feet then, and required constant dredging. Winter storms left a bar at the entrance that had to be removed each spring at the start of the shipping season and sometimes the dredge even had to return in the fall as lake level's dropped to deepen the channel again.

Range Light at inner end of west pier   around 1918 with young George Green, Edna Williams, and possibly their aunt. Fair Haven at this time had a light on each end of its long western jetty. Both were serviced by a keeper whose house was located on a knoll just west of the barrier bar. He used a boat to reach the lights on occasion kept at a boathouse where now the Boat House Marina operates. The inner range was deactivated around 1945 and the last keeper of the lights was Osgar Elmer.

The Bay View Hotel located at the end of 10th Street on the eastern side of Fair Haven Bay. This was a popular spot for vacationing anglers. Judging from the long dresses on the two women this was taken well before 1920. The lower part of the building served as a storage area and boat shop with the rooms to rent above. The large launch tied up outside the little boat basin was used for excursions on the bay.

Fair Haven has a long history as a resort area. As early as 1859 an inn on the lakeshore was catering to the summer trade and after the rail connection to the south was completed in the 1870's tourists from Auburn and Syracuse became a staple of the summer economy here, as they still are to this day. There were four waterfront hotels on the bay in the early 1900's.

An unknown pair of boaters enjoy an outing on the bay probably before 1920. They are aboard one of Burt Card's rental boats obtained at the Bay View Hotel and it's likely they are not far from that establishment, somewhere along the east shore of the bay.

The large wooden structure behind them is probably one of the several large ice houses that then fronted the bay near the present location of Grant's Trailer Park. In the early 1900's ice cutting was for over a decade a major winter employment for Fair Haven area fishermen and trestle workers connected with the port during navigation season. For over a decade an annual harvest of 79,000 tons was stored away in these houses insulated by saw dust or marsh grass. The business declined rapidly in the 1920's once artificial ice replaced the bay's product.

Burt Card was one of several boat builders on the bay. This light model pulling boat would slip along nicely on a calm bay with little effort. Note the pinned oars. These were the customary style on the south shore bays of the lake and on the St. Lawrence River where trolling for a fish was a primary reason for rowing. When you got a bite, you could drop the oars and play your catch and not worry about losing either the fish or the oars.

130

The rental rowboat fleet on a quiet day at the state park. Are the two gentlemen awaiting a customer?

The park opened around 1928 with the dock in the bay where these skiffs appear to be tied being built a few years later by CCC crew. The boats are quite different from Burt Card's model- they are clinker planked and double ended and look like typical St. Lawrence skiffs probably produced by one of the larger shops on the river. Several shops on the St. Lawrence turned them out on a production basis through the 1930's- they were fairly heavy because such skiffs were never portaged and their weight made them more stable to move around in and easy to keep moving in a bit of a chop. Note the skiff chairs in the stern that could be removed and used as back rests on the beach. The big shops made rowing boats in several grades according to intended use- a commercial rental grade skiff would have iron clinch nails and iron hardware and a painted finish while a fancy grade boat would feature figured wood end decks, a varnished hull and interior and

Fair Haven Beach State Park shortly after it opened around 1928. The park was popular with summer visitors right from the start with up to 10,000 people and 3000 cars present on a hot July Sunday in the 1930's. Not until after 1934 did CCC workers stabilize the channel between the Lake and the pond that the swimmers are enjoying here. When the park first opened it maintained a dress code for bathers that called for covering those manly torsos. It's difficult to imagine what the ladies had to try to swim in back in those days. Maybe that's why we don't see any women in the water in this photo.

Note the actively eroding park bluff face in the background, since stabilized with toe protection boulders and partially vegetated

Pleasant Beach Hotel probably shortly after it opened in 1910

There's a fine westerly blowing on this summer day, are the folks on the lawn perhaps watching a boat race? They all seem to be looking the same way. With the generous flag display and the apparent early growth in the rhubarb could this perhaps be Flag Day in June on the bay?

young George Green and two cousins Ida and Harley Stevenson by the bay "messing with boats" about 1918

George at the oars is a bit older here. His simple "flat iron" skiff was probably made locally as at least two boat shops were in business then on the bay.

Perhaps a quarter century after the day rowing on the bay with his cousins, George takes his Robin for a sail.

Further passages on inland waters

Below in no particular order are some passages, recent and out of print on Lake Ontario and adjoining inland waters that I have found enjoyable.

Tales From The Great Lakes by Robert Townsend 1995; Canadian historian and yachtsman Robert Townsend has done sailors and history buffs alike a great service by editing and organizing some of the more than 1300 "schooner Days" columns published by C. H. J. Snider in the *Toronto Evening Telegram* a between 1931 and 1956. As far as I know this is the only such collection published to date. Townsend has included photos of ships and some of Snider's wonderful artwork.

Captain John Williams, Master Mariner Also by Robert Townsend 2001; Another compilation of Snider's columns organized to form the biography of a Lake Ontario schoonerman who successfully transitioned to steam. His sea going career began at age nine in 1866 and ended in 1927, and he never lost a man or a ship during his days as a captain.

Tarry Breeks and Velvet Garters C.H.J. Snider 1958; Townsend calls Snider Canada's greatest maritime historian. Fortunately for Lake Ontario history buffs he lived and sailed for much of his long life on the body of water generally overlooked in most anthologies on our inland seas by American writers. He also sailed on working lake schooners as crew and on the salt bankers including the *Bluenose*. This book deals with the history of French sail on the lakes and also tells of Rene Hypolite La Force, a real life Aubry-Hornblower who was a diplomat and translator to the Indian tribes, a successful salt water ship owner and sea captain, a military scout and expert woodsman, and as Snider puts it "first Canadian Commodore Twice over" of the French and then the British Provincial Marine. He had an astonishing career and Snider says it was either he or possibly his brother who was described by George Washington as an enemy who would do more disservice than fifty other men".

In The Wake of the Eighteen Twelvers C.H.J.Snider 1913; Described as a novel I'd characterize it as an example of what is now called creative nonfiction. Snider subtitles it Fights and flights of frigates and fore-n-afters on the lakes and he says he clothes the dry bones of record with the flesh and blood of fancy. He has been factual on the battle maneuvers, the gear, the names of ships and men involved, and the numbers of casualties which in some of these freshwater battles were appalling. In one battle the British lost 50 killed or wounded from a ship's company of 125. The book is enhanced by Snider's accurate artwork depicting some of the warships.

The Pathfinder by James Fenimore Cooper 1840; Set during the French and Indian War on the shores of Lake Ontario. Cooper served in Oswego under Woolsey but resigned just before the war started. The Pathfinder deals with skirmishes and battles and follows the cutter Scud and her young captain eau-douce across the waves.

The Living Great Lakes Jerry Dennis 2003; A recent well written account of a delivery passage from Lake Michigan to Maine aboard a 74 ton gaff rigged schooner. Not much on Lake Ontario, two chapters on the ship's salt water travels, lots of good history and cruising on the upper lakes.

Away Jane Urquhart 1993; This Canadian writer follows a family of Irish immigrants through several generations. The last of the family ends up on the lakeshore next to a cement quarry and watches the lake chew away her farm while the quarry eats up the land next door. Lake Ontario makes a brief appearance, but the author captures life on the edge with great eloquence.

In The Wake Of The Gemini Ann Davison 1962 This 6000 mile voyage in an outboard boat from Miami up the ICW through and back down the Mississippi includes the Hudson, Erie Canal and Trent Severn and lake Michigan. Davison's previous books detailed her solo trans Atlantic trip with a 23 foot sloop and her first sea voyage during which things went terribly wrong. This early British bird aviator and adventurer has an interesting perspective on our inland waters. I think this was her last book as after this cruise she swallowed the anchor and remarried and we assume no longer needed to put bread on the table with her very capable pen.

And,

there are numerous websites dealing with aspects of the Great Lakes including my own *Log On Line* located at www.silverwaters.com

Other books by the author

The Edge Walker's Guide to Lake Ontario Beach combing 157 page paperback photos, illustrations by author $17.00 Where to go and what to look for along the public shorelines of Lake Ontario with maps, natural history notes and photos.

Mirages Monsters Myths and Mysteries of Lake Ontario 90 page booklet retail $8.50 a collections of legends folklore and stores from old news archives, local histories and memories. Ghosts, Indian tales and shipwrecks of Lake Ontario.

The Great Atomic Lake $8.50 An overview of problems posed to Lake Ontario by ageing commercial nuclear power plants and the potential benefits of sustainable energy production now possible.

Crossing To Canada- Advice for Novice Cruisers Traveling Lake Ontario 33 page booklet $5.00

Fair Haven Bay Natural History Auto/Cycle Tour pamphlet $2.00

To order these or to learn more about Silver Waters Sailing visit www.silverwaters.com or e mail the author at susan@silverwaters.com snail mail orders can go to 12025 Delling Road, Wolcott NY 14590 315 594 1906 please add two dollars for books, one dollar for booklet and pamphlet postage

About The Author

Susan Peterson Gateley is a native upstate New Yorker who single handed the wooden sloop "Ariel" in search of stories for boating and nature magazines for 17 years. In 1996 she acquired a different boat and partner and added Gateley to her name. Her articles about Lake Ontario have run in numerous local and national publications including the *Buffalo News, Rochester Democrat & Chronicle, Canadian Yachting, Lakeland Boating, Countryside* and others. She has a masters degree in fisheries science and has worked in Massachusetts and on the Chesapeake Bay as an ichthyoplankton taxonomist.

She has crewed on sailing yachts in the Caribbean and offshore and has written on topics ranging from angora cats to apples while working at a variety of jobs, several of which were directly or indirectly related to Lake Ontario. These included fresh fruit scout, QC cannery worker, and fire watch at Ginna, giving her an unusual perspective on the lake which she has shared with readers of her four full length nonfiction books and two booklets on Lake Ontario. She also publishes the Lake Ontario Log an e zine available at www.silverwaters.com.

Peterson Gateley holds a Coast Guard license to 25 ton and operates Silver Waters Sailing offering day trips over night excursions and sailing instruction and liveaboard courses aboard a classic 32 foot Sparkman & Stephens sloop on Fair Haven Bay. Visit www.silverwaters.com for more information on other publications.